What People Are Saying About
"DOING IT ALL ISN'T EVERYTHING"

"Women are constantly being told how to do this and how to be that. Enough! **Doing It All Isn't Everything** is long overdue. It's a book to be reread, not loaned out—a friend. Steffie Allen and Carolyn Zeiger are beacons of common sense—I thank them both.**"**

> —Dr. Judith Briles
> Author, *The Confidence Factor* and
> *Woman to Woman*

"In these pages there is a celebration of being a woman—with joy experienced every step along the way. The message is clear: take care of yourself and you will be able to do anything you choose to do.**"**

> —Dr. Lenore Walker
> Domestic violence expert, speaker, and author
> of *The Battered Woman* and *Terrifying Love*

"This insightful, thought-provoking book encourages the reader to make choices, seize control, change, and grow.**"**

> —Marilyn Van Derbur Atler
> Activist working with adult survivors
> of childhood sexual abuse, Named
> Outstanding Woman Speaker in America

"A fantastic book to help women honor the feminine and avoid burnout.**"**

> —Dottie Lamm
> Columnist, speaker, and former
> "First Spouse" of Colorado

*d*oing It All
isn't
EVERYTHING

Steffie (l.)
and Carolyn (r.),
Buffalo Creek, Colorado
July , 1947

Carolyn (l.)
and Steffie (r.)
Denver, Colorado
July, 1992

The Allen Sisters

*d*oing It All *isn't* EVERYTHING

A Woman's Guide to Harmony and Empowerment

CAROLYN ALLEN ZEIGER, Ph.D.

STEPHANIE ALLEN

with

Liz Netzel

A BARD PRODUCTIONS BOOK

NEW PERSPECTIVES PRESS

Doing It All Isn't Everything
A Woman's Guide to Harmony and Empowerment

Copyright © 1993 by Carolyn Allen Zeiger and Stephanie Allen

New Perspectives Press
5275 McCormick Mountain Drive
Austin, Texas 78734
512-266-2112   FAX 512-266-2749

Quantity discounts are available. Please contact the publisher as listed above.

Cloth edition: ISBN 0-9632788-1-9
Trade paperback edition: ISBN 0-9632788-0-0

The authors may be contacted through: The Athena Group
1780 S. Bellaire St.,
Suite 506
Denver, CO 80222
303/782-5060

A BARD PRODUCTIONS BOOK
AUSTIN, TEXAS

Copyediting: **Helen Hyams**

Text Design: **Suzanne Pustejovsky**

Jacket Design: **Suzanne Pustejovsky**

Composition/Production: **Round Rock Graphics**

TABLE OF CONTENTS

7

DEDICATION

To all the women
who have come before us;
to all the women
who accompany us now on this journey;
to all the women
who will follow us;
and especially to our mother,
Margot Hart Tettemer,
who has nurtured and sustained us always

OUR PARTNERSHIP

S tephanie Allen and Carolyn Allen Zeiger, Ph.D., are sisters, born five years apart into a white, upper-middle-class family. An older brother from another marriage, Eddie, went away to boarding school early on in their childhoods, returning home for holidays. Carolyn, the youngest, characterizes the family social standing as "fading gentility." Fourth-generation natives of Denver, Colorado, the family had watched the wealth of the first generation disappear. Without money, the family's social standing was tenuous—but they were still listed in the social register. The sisters' parents held on to their country club membership and friends. This gave the sisters an entrée into the world of civic and social power, yet they didn't have the wherewithal to participate fully. This put them in the interesting position of being both insiders and outsiders, learning the perspectives of the "haves" and the "have nots" at the same time.

Carolyn:

For many years, we lived on a block where the income and social status of the residents ranged from that of a poor, uneducated single mother to families where daddy was a classic upper-middle-class businessman or lawyer who had bought his family a fine house. We were somewhere in between.

My friends included the doctor's sons and Linette, a girl who lived across the street from them in the most run-down house on the block.

After she played at my house, there was often something missing from my room. I finally caught her eating my treasured extra-fat candy cane. For at least a month I had been gnawing on it, taking it down about half an inch a day. I loved knowing that every day I could have a little treat after school and still have something left for the next day. As soon as I noticed that the candy was missing, I ran over to her house. I was so mad when I saw the last little bit sticking out of her mouth. It was practically gone! But after the first flash of righteous rage, I let it go. It suddenly occurred to me that no one had ever given her such a treat. Seeing it in my room day after day was just too big a temptation for her, and of course she had eaten it all at once. I couldn't say anything to her. I just ran back home sobbing in confusion over the unfairness of her unhappy circumstances, pain over the loss of my precious candy cane, and anger at my friend for stealing from me.

Steffie:

Our parents' financial situation kept deteriorating as we got older. When we were teenagers we had to stretch our budgets and our imaginations to get formal dresses to wear to the cotillions and holiday balls. To find a dress we could afford, Carol and I would go to Montaldo's final mark-down sale at the end of the season to buy an outfit for the following year. Then we would modify it two or three times so we wouldn't be wearing the same thing all the time. I enjoyed the challenge and became an accomplished seamstress.

Our efforts to "fit in" to the country club scene also forced us to find ways to make money, which further set us apart from the children of our parents' friends. My passion was horseback riding. To ride in the best shows I trained horses in exchange for riding them in competition and taught the owners'

*children to ride to earn money for entry fees.
Although I was always aware of this state of being
simultaneously on the inside and the outside, I don't
remember feeling resentful. Daddy used to tell us,
"Class isn't about money. It's about what kind of
person you are." Besides, living in more than one
world was interesting. Anyway, it was all we knew.*

Carolyn:

*By the time I was a teenager, even grocery and rent
money was scarce. Mother was working now too, at
several jobs at once. She taught ballet and dancing
school and did bookkeeping and sales for a friend's
"exclusive" women's clothing boutique. Our parents
were constantly fighting and life at home was really
awful. Daddy became more and more "difficult" (our
term for his outrageous, flamboyant, argumentative
behavior). He also drank a lot. Sometimes, he was
withdrawn and gloomy. We later learned that he
suffered from manic-depression, which is genetically
transmitted. Mother was miserable. Steffie wasn't
home much during this period, and I tried not to be.
Then our parents divorced. I was sent to live for a
summer with a great-uncle on Fire Island, then
to relatives in Philadelphia, and finally to boarding
school on borrowed money. Every year I went to a
different school, while Steffie trained horses, taught
dancing school, and custom-knit sweaters to pay for
her college tuition. After she was kicked out of a
restrictive Eastern women's college for breaking the
rules, our parents left it up to her to get through
school on her own.*

*For years, mother apologized for this "terrible
period" in our lives, but now she agrees with us
that, although painful, it was good for all of us. I'm
grateful that I had to learn to be independent and
adaptable, to constantly make new friends, and to
keep on course for college when the classes offered at*

*my new school didn't fit with the sequence of the
last one I went to.*

*Our parents always found a way to give us
what we actually needed, and they passed on strong
values to us, including the importance of education.
We both worked and earned scholarships to help us
through college.*

As Steffie completed college, she began to follow a traditional path. She earned a B.A. degree in history, married
a powerful businessman, had two sons, and developed an
active career as a volunteer, including roles as president of
the Junior League of Denver and founder of regional educational programs and arts expositions.

When her marriage soured, Steffie used her community
connections as a springboard to a new life. After her divorce,
she leaped into a high-powered job as a development director,
raising more than forty million dollars for the University of
Denver. Her career took off, and she went on to serve as a
management development trainer, then as CEO of a management software company, which she took public. In each of
these positions, she strengthened her organization development and leadership skills and earned a reputation for
innovation and vision. Throughout this time, she continued
to serve on many community boards of directors.

Carolyn, meanwhile, blossomed into unconventionality
during her college years. As an undergraduate, she founded
a controversial student newspaper, and she went on to be the
only woman in her graduate school class. She lived briefly
in a commune, sharing a three-bedroom house with twelve
other people; in the forefront of the times, they held marathon
encounter groups and read mystical texts. At this point,
spiritual development became the driving force in her life.

Carolyn also pursued her career wholeheartedly, earn-
ing a Ph.D. degree in clinical psychology in spite of her father,
who told her, "No woman needs a Ph.D." (narrowmindedness
that he later outgrew and apologized for). She created a
multidisciplinary private mental health clinic in Boulder,
Colorado, and was director and clinical supervisor there for

fourteen years. In her professional capacity, she founded two pioneering professional organizations. She also founded and for many years served as director of the Siddha Meditation Center in Boulder. She has taught courses in meditation throughout the western United States.

Divorcing after a short marriage in graduate school, Carolyn later married a computer scientist. They had a daughter together and Carolyn became stepmother to his two children. She and her sister have both taken in foster children who have remained important members of their family circles.

In the early eighties, Steffie was drawn to the notion of leadership. She began to unravel the differences in the ways men and women lead, and to confirm her belief that both the feminine and masculine perspectives would be critical for effective organizations in the next century.

Steffie honed her vision of women being in equal partnership with men and acknowledged that, because of inadequate opportunities in the past, women needed a special boost to be able to do this. Her vision dovetailed with Carolyn's lifelong commitment to helping people experience and live out their inner greatness. Thus, when Steffie approached Carolyn about creating a training company, Carolyn embraced the idea. They have been partners ever since.

Today, Steffie is cochair and founder of a statewide women's leadership coalition and past president of an international organization for distinguished women. She also serves as chair of the ethics committee of a hospital board of directors. Remarried to an environmental advocate, she still seeks adventure outdoors, skiing, fishing, and biking with her husband. She also loves to read.

Carolyn has left her private psychotherapy practice but continues as an adjunct faculty member of the graduate school of the University of Colorado, where she trains and supervises graduate students. In her spare time, she creates imaginative sculpture and writes articles on spirituality in everyday life for *DARSHAN* magazine.

Steffie and Carolyn have survived many of the traumatic life experiences that other people have weathered. Because of a serious learning disability, Steffie couldn't read until she was in junior high school. Spelling bees were a source of enormous humiliation for her. Spelling bees were Carolyn's crowning glory, but health problems have always plagued her. Between them, they have lived through chronic health problems and accidents, the collapse of a business, manic-depressive disorder in two generations, step-family life—as children and as parents—sexual harassment and sexual abuse by strangers, the suicide of a family member, and the loss of a parent to cancer. This book is their way of sharing what they have learned—about surviving and thriving—as they have moved through the stages of growth and change in their own lives.

ACKNOWLEDGMENTS

*I*t isn't possible to identify all the people who contributed to this book. As a famous scientist said, we always build on the shoulders of others. And often we aren't even aware of who those others are. So we thank all of the people, known and unknown, whose lives and work are represented here in some form. This includes all the men and women who have worked with our business through The Athena Group, all the women who read preliminary drafts, our colleagues past and present, and our families.

We especially thank Kay Johnson, who was one of the founders of The Athena Group. She generously shared her life with us in many ways. The book was written at her insistence and she lovingly hounded us to keep at it. Her presence is felt throughout the book, especially in the work related to goals and values.

Those who have included foundational ideas, inspiration, and encouragement include Jackie Frischkneckt, Peter Ossorio, Mary McDermott Shideler, and Warren Ziegler. And supporting all that we do in life are the teachings of Gurumayi Chidvilasananda, whose example shows us all that we can become.

Part One

THE ROOTS
OF THE
QUEST

1

Creating Harmony in Your Life

▲▲To keep our faces toward change and behave like free spirits in the presence of fate is strength undefeatable.**▲▲**

—**Helen Keller**

▲▲Where there is an open mind, there will always be a frontier.**▲▲**

—**Charles F. Kettering**

▲▲There is more to life than increasing its speed.**▲▲**

—**Mahatma Gandhi**

*T*HIS IS A BOOK FOR WOMEN LIKE OURSELVES who want to work but also want more in life than just the job. The "job" may be a lifelong career, a profession (including professional volunteer work), or part-time or occasional work at different times during your life. The "something else" in life may be family, a sport, a political cause, a love relationship, a spiritual life, a creative hobby— any pursuit that might hold an important place in your existence. We invite you to join us in exploring how to have *both* without wearing yourself out by trying to do it all, without stifling the fullness of your being by focusing too narrowly on one aspect of life or giving up altogether in bitterness or disappointment.

Living life in harmony is a challenge; it is certainly not easy for anybody. It is harder for men in some ways, and harder for women in others. Our focus in this book is on showing how women can become whole, authentic individuals intentionally making choices that support a harmonious life: a life where our multiple roles fulfill us, instead of tearing us apart.

Not so long ago, the feminist battle cry "We can have it all!" became a nearly collective goal for American women. Many of us who moved into business and professional arenas in the sixties and seventies were eager to prove that we were no different from men, could do just as well as men, and, at the same time, could hold on to our roles as caretakers of our mates, children, and aging parents. We were confident that we could, indeed, "have it all."

Yet over time we began to feel a vague, persistent malaise. Something wasn't working out. The thought of juggling multiple roles and demands like superhuman acrobats no longer struck a stirring chord in our spirits as it had two or three decades before. Somehow, no matter how well we did or how much we had, we were feeling more worn-out than successful, more disillusioned than satisfied. These feelings perplexed us. Had we not been up to the task after all? Had we set ourselves to the wrong task? Was there something fundamentally flawed, or missing, in women? Or was there something wrong with our culture that prevented us from having it all no matter how hard we tried?

Columnists, feminists, academicians, business people—and all the rest of us—are busily trying to address these contemporary questions and are coming up with answers ranging from "Women are and always will be the keepers of the hearth and they should just go home" to "The 'old boys' club' still holds the keys to paradise and we just need to fight harder to wrest them away."

In 1989, we created a leadership training organization called The Athena Group to solve gender issues in the workplace. Our position is that men and women can, and for our mutual personal and societal benefit should, work together effectively. With appreciation and respect. With "bottom-line" results. With humor and good times. At home and at work. The "having it all" issue is a complex one to sort out, as are all social problems. Nonetheless, we must take into account two important truths as we pursue the vision of harmony.

First, doing it all is no longer an option. It's no wonder that we're worn out, no surprise that we're left feeling like angry and guilty failures. *It isn't possible to do it all and remain either sane or healthy*—let alone productive or personally fulfilled. Harmony requires us to make choices and reorganize priorities. Our culture needs to allow women to share in the rewards of the traditional male world of business and professional life without having to do everything women traditionally did *on top of* becoming "honorary men" at the office. And the business world needs to incorporate women's ways of being to create a more nurturing and enlivening environment for both men and women.

Second, our attempts to be "just like men" are misguided. We have come to confuse equal opportunity and equal worth with having identical ways of being in the world. Our notion has been that if we are equal in rights and value, we must also be identical in our personal characteristics. Sadly, succeeding in business has often meant imitating men. Likewise, our desire to make men be more like us has failed to solve the problem, although that attitude persists among some women. We have also experimented with the model of androgyny, insisting that both men and women exhibit the same traits and behaviors and maintaining that there really are no differences between the sexes.

It is certainly the case that men and women are more alike than different, but research has revealed substantive differences in some areas. It is important to explore and understand them, for whatever the as-yet-undiscovered source of these differences may be, we must honor and make good use of them.

Businesses are beginning to appreciate the value of racial and cultural diversity. They see now that we can be ourselves and learn from each other as well—to the vast benefit of the organization. This inclusion of different perspectives to enrich the workplace must extend to masculine and feminine perspectives as well.

Given all of this, what can the contemporary woman do? It is painful to think that in some ways we may not have been living authentic lives, that we may not have been true to ourselves. Yet we think that to some extent this is the case. In the last two decades, women in the United States have tried to be and do it all, and our lives have become discordant. Now we need to turn our backs on Superwoman and explore who we are as individual women, to make decisions about what we want, and don't want, to be and do in the world. To accomplish this, we must claim and honor both the masculine and feminine in ourselves. Self-knowledge leads to empowerment, and empowerment is in turn reflected in a harmonious life.

We in no way advocate turning away from the progress women have made in this century or from the political action that has brought it about. Instead, we are talking about strengthening and building upon these gains. As Betty Friedan notes, feminism needs to "transcend sexual politics and anger against men to express a new vision of family and community. We must go beyond the victim's state to mobilizing the new power of women and men for a larger political agenda on the priorities of life" (Blackman, Painton, and Taylor, 1992, p. 55). With a clear knowledge of ourselves as a foundation, each of us can find an arena of activity that suits us. We can then choose a way to achieve a larger measure of personal fulfillment and to participate in the social changes that will allow both men and women to appreciate and fulfill their particular, individual natures. Quite simply, we advocate empowerment for all of the people.

EMPOWERMENT DEFINED

Empowerment consists of being and claiming your authentic self and, in so doing, leading a meaningful and productive life. There is no road map for empowerment. This book is a sharing of lessons we have learned by our midlife from work, family, spiritual masters, loyal friends, and dedicated enemies; from tragedy and triumph; and from foolish fancies—an abundance of life experiences. We have also included the experiences of many other women from our research and our training programs. They represent a rich mix in terms of race, ethnicity, and family and cultural background. For the most part, we chose women over thirty-five to show the course their lives have taken, the difficult choices they have made over time. We have used these older women to stress the point that each of us creates our life, and that takes time. An insidious part of the "doing-it-all" syndrome is the frantic attempt to cram everything into our lives at once. Discovering our inner power is an ongoing endeavor.

Of course, this book is being revised and added to as we go to press and, we hope, indefinitely. We don't expect, or want, you to "believe" what is written here. But we invite you to read, to try out the ideas and perspectives, and to check them against your own life experience.

Although the book is written in the first person, there are two "I's." Sometimes one or the other of us wrote most of a chapter. At other times, we pooled our experiences. There are themes in this book that one of us relates to more strongly than the other. Also, we think differently. Steffie makes sense of her experiences more through stories and colorful images, Carolyn through the use of organizing concepts and carefully chosen words. For the most part, we have gotten used to a working style where we both just jump in and talk, contributing in accordance with our particular styles, until we come up with something we're both excited about—or at least until one can live with what the other insists on. In this same collaborative way, we have blended our voices and our passions in our company, The Athena Group.

Many of the exercises in the book are used in our leadership training program for women, "Empowering Women for Excellence." We began the training program by identifying the qualities of the working women we considered "empowered"—vital, joyful women who were authentic, aligned, and satisfied with their lives—though not perfect, and not necessarily successful by conventional standards.

But also not strung out.

We were careful to exclude bitter, demoralized, or worn-out women who had all the symbols of success, but no sense of fulfillment. We were looking for models whose *inner* attainment we could all emulate.

The women who helped us identify the qualities we sought are quite diverse. Their work is varied and ranges from politics to professional voluntarism to cleaning houses. Their personalities, backgrounds, and interests are equally varied. The majority are white, middle-class, and heterosexual. Although we have not studied all kinds of women in all kinds of situations, we were struck by the consistency of what we saw in the women we did study. The facets of empowerment reflect the qualities we witnessed in all of them. The strength of each quality varied from woman to woman, but each was present in some measure. Since our initial research project, we have worked with this material in training hundreds of women of all ages and racial and socioeconomic groups. These participants confirm our initial observations. We believe that these qualities are needed by every woman and man.

All of us have these empowerment qualities to some degree, but usually we are not aware of them. Yet once we can claim these qualities and deliberately make use of them, we are in a far better position to lead satisfying, fulfilling lives. Of course, all of us are weak in certain areas, too, just as our sample group was. But when we are aware of our weaknesses, we can strengthen those aspects—with compassion as well as discipline and determination. Living in harmony with ourselves, as well as with others, is a lifelong quest.

FROM DOING TO BEING

The process of working toward inner peace must in itself be a gentle one. The usual approach to self-development involves forcing yourself to perform ever greater feats, or requiring yourself to be like somebody else, as if all leaders had identical personalities and visions that one could (and should) assume at will. This is the very Superwoman trap we advocate transcending. Our approach is very different. In the quest for harmony, the shift in focus is from doing to being. We believe that the right actions—the doing—springs from inner wholeness and alignment. Inner harmony is then reflected in an outward harmony.

We see this in the women who have taken our training course. What they report most often is an increase in self-esteem and self-confidence. They talk about a sense of relief, about liking themselves more and feeling better about their lives, and about having new focus and direction. In addition, they tell us that these positive changes in their self-assessment have been translated into changes in the way they live, at work and at home. Claiming ourselves is much more important than building skills per se. Skills are only helpful if they are developed in response to our sense of who we are and where we are going.

This is not a simplistic, "everybody's okay just as they are so let's congratulate ourselves and go back to sleep" approach. Self-inquiry is critical. The inner greatness we all share is nurtured and revealed more clearly as we strengthen our good habits and replace the poor ones with new, better ones. On the other hand, there's no need to carry on endless self-flagellation in the name of growth. Note your weaknesses and get to work. But give yourself time and show yourself loving encouragement along the way.

USING THIS BOOK

In this book, we have tried to provide as many tools as possible for you to use in cultivating the qualities of empowerment and establishing harmony in your life. As you will see, these tools include journal writing, meditation, and a variety of exercises you can do either alone or with others.

Some of the facets of empowerment will strike a chord for you and some may not. Use what is helpful and disregard the rest. As you read through each chapter, highlight those qualities of empowerment in which you are skilled, the ones you consider to be well developed. These are the qualities you can count on when they're needed. Congratulate yourself. Celebrate! Notice where these qualities serve you well in life, and where you could make better or more frequent use of them. See whether you want to use any of the exercises to further enhance these qualities. Make up your own exercises.

When you discover a facet of empowerment you feel is weak, reread that chapter. Think about what difference it would make in your life to cultivate this quality. Think specifically about areas where a lack of the quality is hurting you. Consider all areas of your life. Use the exercises to develop the desired qualities and to gain practice and experience by putting your new skills and understanding to use. Again, make up your own exercises for developing these qualities. As a further reinforcement, read biographies and autobiographies of women you admire; literature provides many powerful role models.

As you become more empowered, you will become more comfortable with your own nature. You will find it easier to make choices and will feel more contented with those choices. You will clearly understand how to bring your various roles into a harmonious whole—the life you are creating for yourself, as only you can.

We encourage you to come back and reread this book in the future. You will have changed in the meantime; maybe something will strike you differently then or speak to you in a new way. We hope that this book stimulates your thinking—and feeling. We hope that it inspires you to stretch and grow. One final caution: Don't transfer a Superwoman mind-set from "doing it all" to "being everything." Creating a harmonious life is the goal.

2

Empowering Yourself

❙❙ *All serious daring starts from within.* **❙❙**
—**Eudora Welty**

❙❙ *We carry within us the wonders we seek without us.* **❙❙**
—**Sir Thomas Browne**

❙❙ *He who rides a tiger is afraid to dismount.* **❙❙**
—**Chinese proverb**

*T*HE ESSENCE OF THIS BOOK IS EMPOWERMENT. We repeat our concept of empowerment here: *Empowerment is claiming and being your authentic self and, in so doing, leading a meaningful and productive life.* The aim of this book is to help you to understand and embrace your true self, and to create a plan of action for leading a life that allows you to be the best person you can be, in the way that only you can.

Being empowered requires laying a foundation of contemplation, commitment, conviction, and courage:

- *Contemplation.* A vital feature of an examined life, contemplation involves taking time out from your life on a regular basis to explore its meaning. One way in which women avoid full empowerment is by staying too busy for introspection. This is like walking across the country and only looking at the yellow line on the highway. That single-minded focus on the tasks at hand makes for a dull journey through life. By experiencing life and then reflecting on your experiences, you can gain an intimate sense of the significance of your existence. Contemplation drives actions, decisions, and values that equate eventually to wisdom, change, and growth.

- *Commitment.* With a clear sense of yourself, you are in a position to commit to your own empowerment, which means that you identify it as something you want to have—something you will dedicate time, learn skills, and take risks to achieve.

- *Conviction.* This quality allows you to stand up to people who try to dissuade you from being yourself. Conviction is the inner knowledge that you don't have to compromise your true essence.

- *Courage.* The empowered woman needs the courage to be disciplined, to stay fit, to make sacrifices, and to endure pain. Having the courage to be yourself fully brings you joy.

Alexis de Tocqueville said that the great flaw in the American dream is the belief that the pursuit of happiness is the purpose of life. Life is not about happiness, but about meaning and purpose. Questing endlessly for happiness leaves us at the mercy of whatever is around us and blinds us to many significant learning experiences. In addition, the search for happiness makes life very one-dimensional. True inner peace goes beyond happiness.

Here are a few more things to remember about empowerment:

- It is a journey along a path, not a destination. Like physical fitness or sound nutrition, it is an ongoing framework for living.

- It changes form and direction and shifts as you grow.

- It is a natural evolutionary process. All human beings begin life powerless and go through stages of greater empowerment throughout their lives, as they continue to recognize and tap into greater power within themselves.

Remember, empowerment comes from within. Empowerment is about becoming who you can be—fully and joyfully—and celebrating your life and all that comes with it. It includes the following facets:

- *Authenticity*—knowing who you are
- *Risk taking*—using your knowledge, experience, and competence
- *Vision*—seeing what is and what could be
- *Health*—using your energy wisely
- *Humor*—approaching life with a light heart
- *Harmony*—bringing your many roles into harmony
- *Receptivity*—having an open mind
- *Accountability*—taking responsibility for your life
- *Contentment*—experiencing love and joy
- *Graciousness*—being comfortable to be around

- *Alignment*—aligning your thoughts, feelings, actions, and values
- *Communication*—communicating well with others
- *Versatility*—working effectively with men and women

Chapters Four through Sixteen are each devoted to one of these facets. First, though, we want to talk about a key theme of our work, our approach, and this book: recognizing, utilizing, and celebrating the differences between the masculine and feminine perspectives and styles.

3

The Masculine and Feminine Perspectives

❚❚In our civilization, men are afraid they will not be men enough and women are afraid that they might be considered only women.**❚❚**

—**Theodor Reik**

❚❚Yet if any human being is to reach full maturity both the masculine and feminine sides of the personality must be brought up into consciousness.**❚❚**

—**M. Esther Harding**

❚❚Male and female are really two cultures and their life experiences are utterly different.**❚❚**

—**Kate Millett**

YOUR PERSPECTIVE IS THE WAY YOU LOOK at the world. Rather than being something you slip in and out of, it is a constant, unconscious framework for making sense of absolutely everything in your life. Although it operates whether you think about it or not, coloring your reactions, impressions, and experiences, you *can* train yourself to become aware of your perspective and to recognize how it influences your decisions and actions.

We like to think of perspective as a lovely, complex tapestry, into which are woven many threads of different colors and textures. The threads of your perspective include your country of origin, your culture, your generation, where you live, your race, and your family traditions. These and other aspects of your point of view allow you to define and claim your individuality and also to connect with others who share your perspective on certain issues.

Our gender is one of the most significant factors affecting our perspective. Think of it as being the foundation of the tapestry—the warp and weft of fabric through which all the other elements are threaded, including your beliefs and your values.

THE CASE FOR DIFFERENCES

When Carolyn was in training in the 1960s, the field of psychology paid little attention to the question of whether there were differences in the psychological makeup of men and women. There were also few women in the field. In the 1970s, as more women were becoming psychologists, the question of male-female differences was raised as a legitimate issue for study. In the political and emotional climate of that time, there was almost a presumption that if men and women had equal rights to compete in the workplace, they must also have the same personal characteristics and abilities. Carolyn certainly felt that way.

In support of this notion, as the research in this area became more and more refined, fewer and fewer differences were found. Two respected psychologists, Carol Jacklin and Eleanor Maccoby, conducted a thorough review of studies that compared males and females of all ages on personality traits, such as independence and dependence, and on abilities, such as mathematical and verbal skills (Jacklin and Maccoby, 1974). They found very few consistent differences between the sexes, and those they did find were small. Overall, in terms of individual personality characteristics and individual abilities, their review of the research showed that males and females (boys and girls as well as men and women) are much more alike than different.

But are we really alike in all respects? Experiences in our own lives make it hard to believe that we're all on the same wavelength. There are too many awkward, painful miscommunications, clashing agendas, and relationship struggles between men and women for this to be so. This was very evident to Carolyn when she practiced psychotherapy with couples. By the late 1980s, evidence from diverse sources that was accumulating showed that in some respects, men and women function very differently. (The question "Why?" is one we'll get to later.) Eleanor Maccoby was once more one of the key researchers on this subject. She suspected that researchers had not been asking the right questions. What matters, she suggested, is what males and females are like in their interactions with others—how they behave in relationships. With this in mind, Dr. Maccoby reviewed a mass of research literature describing how males and females of all ages actually behave in groups (Maccoby, 1990).

Reviewing the studies with this focus revealed clear and consistent differences starting at least in preschool and extending through adolescence and adulthood. This issue has been, and continues to be, highly emotionally charged. Ideas of "political correctness" also influence what people think and say. Our work is based on what we see as the best data at hand, and we want to share some of this information with you.

Dr. Maccoby's findings can be described in terms of two key differences:

1. Differing means of establishing one's personal identity, or differences in the ways we go about defining and claiming who we are

2. Differing ways in which males and females go about influencing others' behavior

The male orientation is to establish a separate personal identity through competition and dominance as contrasted with the female orientation toward achieving an identity based on connection with others—through affirmation of, and cooperation with, others. That is, a male feels affirmed as a worthwhile person by competing to stand out from the group as an individual (the "best" sportsman, student, and so on). A female feels affirmed as a person when she is successful in establishing her place within a community by cooperating with and supporting others (as a caretaker, social facilitator, and so on). The male focus is on separation from others; the female focus is on connection.

In keeping with their orientation toward claiming personal identity, males are likely to use direct commands to attempt to change someone's behavior (as they pursue dominance), whereas females make polite requests or suggestions (as they pursue relationships). In other words, males give orders, and females offer possibilities to be considered.

How is this played out? Needless to say, the gentle, facilitative female influence style is highly effective with other females who have the shared objective of creating and sustaining stable relationships. That is, a woman is highly effective at furthering her individual desires, as well as achieving group cohesion, when she is with other women. Likewise, the male style works for men when they are with other men. Obviously, these different agendas and ways of accomplishing them are at cross-purposes when men and women get together. In that case, the male command-and-control style usually wins out.

In terms of relationships, the trade-offs are clear. Men trade intimacy for power over others, and women trade power over others for intimacy. Each approach has its payoffs and downsides.

A number of researchers in different fields, working independently, have discovered basically the same descriptions of how men and women behave in social interactions. For further information on this topic, some interesting books are *You Just Don't Understand* by linguist Deborah Tannen (1990); *In a Different Voice* by psychologist Carol Gilligan (1982), which covers differing perspectives in moral judgments; *Workforce America* by business researchers Marilyn Loden and Judy B. Rosner (1991), on the management and leadership styles of men and women; *The Female Advantage,* journalist Sally Helgeson's (1990) case study of successful businesswomen; and *Women of Influence, Women of Vision* by education professors Helen Astin and Carole Leland (1991), a cross-generational study of leaders and social change. Yes, they are all written by women. That seems to be who's most interested in this subject, and women now have access to training and positions that allow them to explore it. Not all of these researchers set out looking for differences between men and women, nor did they begin with ideas about the kind of differences they might find. Nonetheless, they kept coming up with the same descriptions of differing masculine and feminine perspectives.

So, back to the question "Why?" What is the source of these gender differences? This topic is even more emotionally loaded than the question of whether or not differences exist! We certainly have to explore the part played by physiology. Research is being done, for example, to explore the effect of hormones on the brain. We also have to look at the influence of social forces. Do the differences stem from our relationship with our parents? Our peers? Our whole culture? It is very likely that both biology and the environment come into play here to some extent.

At this point, we simply don't know all the answers. We do know that the brain is highly adaptable and we certainly can, and do, learn to behave in ways that are contrary to our preferred, automatic, "natural" ways. Many women who have succeeded in business have a natural masculine perspective that has enabled them to do well. Others have learned to operate from the masculine worldview, while some use their feminine perspective successfully to operate in what is an alien environment for them. Still others stagger around confused by what is going on around them. Likewise, many men who work in traditional caretaking environments, such as parenting or nursing, have successfully taken on a feminine perspective, and some haven't. Some men operate from the feminine perspective first and then go back and forth between the two points of view.

Our experience is that recognizing, acknowledging, and having a conscious understanding of these differences in perspective is an important component of empowerment that has significant implications for how we understand ourselves and others.

INDEPENDENCE VERSUS RELATEDNESS

It is really quite wonderful news that there are differences, because it explains centuries of strife and misunderstanding. What follows are some further differences in the framework that men and women use to explain the world—those things that distinguish each of our tapestries.

Traditionally, the masculine perspective honors independence and the feminine perspective honors relatedness. In the male perspective, the individual defines himself as autonomous, separate, and concerned with achieving status and recognition—alone. By contrast, in the feminine perspective, the individual defines herself in terms of connection, relationships, and responsibility for others.

In history, the male perspective, which favors individual rights, is epitomized by the U.S. Constitution and the Bill of Rights. Although no equally clear statement of women's values leaps out of the history books, the feminine perspective has traditionally been played out in church and civic activities. The focus on the obligation to others has inspired a diversity of charitable enterprises and grass-roots organizations. Whereas the moral stance of men has to do with individual rights, the moral stance of women has to do with conflicting responsibilities and conflicting relationships. Women are natural spokespersons for the environmental and human rights movements, where the issues have to do with responsibility to the earth and to others. It is here where we have demonstrated leadership during the last three decades.

It should be noted at the outset that neither perspective is superior to the other. Quite the contrary. For it is in the dynamic interaction between the two perspectives that true greatness and achievement for humanity as a whole is realized. Every person has the potential for being all that he or she can be (masculine perspective) *and* for being in a responsible and caring relationship with the outside world (feminine perspective). Either perspective lived to the extreme can be harmful. A person who is entirely selfish may abuse power, exploit others, and exploit the earth. One who is entirely selfless may give up power and fail utterly to live up to his or her individual potential.

It should be clear by now that to be the kind of human being that countless philosophies revere as a model of enlightenment, we must respect and honor both the masculine and the feminine perspectives—in ourselves as well as in others. Beyond that, we must strive to be aware of both perspectives at any given time, and to recognize when each is appropriate to the situation at hand.

Usually we do a constant balancing act between these opposing drives. In business, for example, the drive to make a profit often conflicts with the drive to create a work community that enriches and sustains employees. At home, children are taught the seemingly contradictory values of standing up for themselves (developing into worthy beings) and showing kindness and concern for others (supporting the interests of the group). On a global scale, a classic antagonism divides those who want to develop land for individual profit and those who want to preserve it for everyone to enjoy.

Yet human growth comes out of this tension. People don't become great by having everything their way. Struggling to find a balance between these two perspectives builds character; as we grow, we each develop a sense of self, personal power, and leadership.

SPANNING THE SPECTRUM

Learning to appreciate and use the masculine perspective is different from "becoming just like men." Instead, it is a way of broadening and enriching our own perspective. In the North American culture, the strength of the masculine perspective is manifested when a man is allowed and encouraged to be all that he can be and then extends the values that formed him to society at large. In other words, once a man has settled in and established his independent identity, in the best of cases, he can act on the belief that everyone should benefit from the things he values or has benefited from—whether it is having a good education, being a fine craftsman or athlete, or seeing nature at its best. The challenge for those with a primarily masculine perspective is to find and embrace *a connection with others.*

On the other hand, the strength of the feminine perspective is fulfilled when a woman can meet her need for connectedness and relationship with others *and* go forward to pursue her vision through individual action. For example, women who have successfully raised families may go on to make enormous contributions to cherished causes by emerging as spokespersons and leaders. This may happen in the reverse order, or simultaneously, but both aspects of personality need to be developed. The challenge for those with a primarily feminine perspective is to learn to deal with the real-world issues of control, power, and experience by throwing themselves into *an individual quest for achievement.*

AWAY WITH ANDROGYNY

Please note: Each perspective has a continuum within it. All men are not alike, nor are all women. An individual's perspective may not encompass the entirety of the masculine or the feminine perspective. An individual woman will have some aspects of the masculine perspective, and an individual man some aspects of the feminine. Do not mistake differences for stereotypes.

We're not talking about androgyny here. Earlier, we noted that a balance of perspectives creates a healthy dynamic of tension. Pursuing that analogy, androgyny is a rubber band that has lost all its zip. Men and women have to preserve their preferred perspective and the drive that comes with it *and* understand the perspective of the other sex in order to generate the healthy tension and energy required for creative results.

Part Two

THE FACETS

OF

EMPOWERMENT

4

Authenticity:

KNOWING WHO YOU ARE

❯❯ When she stopped conforming to the conventional picture of femininity she finally began to enjoy being a woman. **❯❯**

—**Betty Friedan**

❯❯ Until you make peace with who you are, you'll never be content with what you have. **❯❯**

—**Doris Mortman**

❯❯ If you always do what interests you, then at least one person is pleased. **❯❯**

—**advice to**
Katharine Hepburn
from her mother

*H*OW WELL DO YOU KNOW YOURSELF? I was once asked to address this question in a very intimidating way. For a project I was working on, I desperately wanted to enlist the help of a world-renowned expert on visioning. To this end, I had charmed my way into a meeting with him. En route to my appointment with this illustrious gentleman, I found I was growing anxious. As I walked through the garden to the carriage house where he had his office, I wondered what he would be like in person. Over the phone he had been crisp, though friendly, and definitely in command of a learned vocabulary. He had a loud, dignified voice—one that movie producers would be pleased to use for the trumpeting voice of God!

Sure enough, he was an imposing person face-to-face; barrel-chested and black-haired, with a touch of defiance in his eyes. I felt reassured, however, when he offered me a cup of tea and settled me in a comfortable chair. Then, suddenly, he leaned across his desk, looked me in the eye, and said, "Who *are* you?" Shades of Dorothy meeting the Wizard of Oz.

I knew in an instant that I had to answer the question from the deepest part of myself if I were to gain this man's respect, let alone his help. In fact, it felt like a rehearsal for that big meeting in the sky with Saint Peter—if I ever got that far. It was clear that my oh-so-beguiling charm could take me no farther. Now I had to get real. He wanted to know the very essence of my *soul*. So I started, and in an uncensored flow, my cherished dreams, deepest fears, and most moving spiritual experiences came forth for our mutual review.

This shared self-inquiry went on for two intense hours. When it was over, I left the meeting stronger, wiser, and happier for the encounter. It forced me to crystallize my thoughts about myself and what I held most dear. In the process, I realized how important it is for each of us to be able to distill and articulate our essential aspects, in order to be effective in the world.

—*Steffie*

THE HEART OF IT ALL

Think of authenticity as being the very center of the multifaceted gem of empowerment. Like the heart of a diamond, authenticity is reflected in every other facet. When we are empowered we exhibit, through our actions, manner, and body language, a deep sense of comfort with who we are. Rather than fostering an exaggerated sense of pride, being authentic allows us to be at home with ourselves, to laugh at ourselves, and to put others at ease.

When we are open and realistic about our capabilities, we may say things like "I'm just not made that way" or "That's not in my nature" or "I'm good at x but doing y bores me to tears." Such self-awareness includes the ability to identify and acknowledge the areas where we need to learn, change, or improve.

A WORK-IN-PROGRESS

Authenticity means understanding the richness and complexity of your true self. It includes an awareness of how you make decisions and organize your world, whether you work well with others, what your values are, what you could drop from your life if you were to add something new, where you are willing to spend your time, and what risks you are willing to take.

Implicit in knowing who you are and who you are not is an understanding of who you *aspire to be*. It is a process that is ever unfolding as you grow and change. You continually incorporate new information you have learned about yourself, updating your self-perception to reflect current reality, adding new skills, and acknowledging areas that are not your forte. For the empowered woman, acknowledgment of self comes easily, without fear, self-reprobation, or guilt.

SIFTING THE WHEAT FROM THE CHAFF

You cannot be all things to all people, though many women try! The goal is to be able to focus your energy on the things that give you joy and satisfaction, and to be able to talk about these things with enthusiasm and conviction. Your goals will vary from year to year and decade to decade as you and your life circumstances change.

Easily, without apology, you accept your areas of weakness. Once, in a group of women, we heard one of the leaders say, "I'm good at asking hard questions, but I lay no claim to finding the answers." One of her colleagues piped up, "We'll make a good team, because I love finding the answer, once I know the question." Like two bookends, these women formed a partnership from which everyone in the group benefited.

THEORY AND PRACTICE

Authenticity requires introspection. Remember, you know yourself better than anyone else does. You need to devote some serious reflective time to unearthing both your strengths and the areas where you are not as strong. This process of discovery leads you through a scrupulous examination of your thoughts, feelings, and values, and shows you how they fit together. Sometimes one or more of these elements may be out of alignment; nonetheless, if you are operating from an authentic stance, you are aware of their proper position when you are at your best, and you regularly and comfortably slip into the role of objective critic of yourself.

In addition to looking within for self-understanding, you must look outside of yourself for data to confirm or deny your own self-perceptions, realizing that others may see things you are blind to in yourself. And to gain constructive feedback, you must create an environment in which others are comfortable.

Finally, all the self-knowledge in the world is virtually worthless until it is translated into actions that direct your life. The key to empowerment is the ability to parlay a keen understanding of your true strengths and weaknesses into an active, challenging life.

Payoffs for Authenticity

▶ **You honor yourself by saying yes and no appropriately.**

▶ **You make sound choices.**

▶ **You choose how you present yourself in a given situation.**

▶ **You build powerful teams.**

▶ **You feel comfortable taking a stand.**

Authenticity in Action

Mary Pacheco has been true to herself and her values throughout a lifetime fraught with tribulations. Extreme hardships and deprivations have sorely limited her opportunities. However, her ability to make the best of whatever life offered has never waned. Although her path in life has not yielded the traditional trappings of success, she fairly glows with inner contentment.

Mary's parents immigrated to the United States illegally and it took many years for the family to move out of a life of fear. Her father was jailed on illegal immigration charges. Later, her mother went to a sanatorium with tuberculosis. At times the children lived with various relatives or took care of their invalid mother. This meant they had to learn at an early age to keep house and to earn a living. With her younger brothers and sisters in tow, Mary went door-to-door looking for someone who would hire a sixteen-year-old to clean house, the same thing her mother had done at the age of eleven. As an adult, she received training and worked for years as a midwife and nurse's aide—work she greatly enjoyed.

Now in her fifties, Mary has returned to housecleaning as a living and it is still a family enterprise. She runs a cleaning service that employs and supports her extended family. It allows her family flexibility in working out care arrangements for elderly, sick, and disabled family members and small children. It provides backup work when other jobs fail. Her work is of such high quality that she can always expand or reduce the workload as family needs vary.

Her business is truly a service. A devout Christian, Mary believes in being a servant of God, and to this end she serves people in many ways. She sees that a home is cleaned thoroughly and lovingly, and she leaves behind the feeling of a peaceful sanctuary. Through her church she runs prayer groups for healing and provides support and direct assistance to recent immigrants from Mexico.

Mary is a cheerful, good-natured person with a calm strength that permeates everything she does. Her Spanish heritage has given her a love of cooking, a strong sense of responsibility for her family, and high regard for hard work. Her self-esteem is solid: She will not work for anyone who doesn't treat her workers respectfully. She has no interest in being well known, having a job in a corporation, or making a lot of money. She constantly expresses her faith that God will provide, her gratitude for whatever comes her way, and her contentment with having "enough."

TOOLS OF EMPOWERMENT

Exercise   *THE "I AM/I AM NOT" CHECKLIST*

Draw a line down the middle of a blank sheet of paper from top to bottom. Label the left-hand column "I Am" and the right-hand column "I Am Not." In the appropriate column describe yourself in words or phrases, without using roles or titles. Here is an example:

I Am	I Am Not
I am a person with a good education in liberal arts and domestic law.	I am not a person who enjoys working with complex business issues.
I am fond of small children and caring for them.	I am not good with teenagers.
I am a good writer.	I am not a good public speaker.
I am an organized person who is good with details.	I am not good at seeing the big picture all the time.
I am good at getting people to work together.	I am not good at inspiring people to take on difficult new assignments.
I am a serious person.	I am not a lighthearted person.
I have high standards for myself and others.	I am not a forgiving person.
I am someone who loves playing and listening to music.	I am not a good storyteller, but I love a good story.

After you have completed the list, put it away for several days. Set aside another time to review and refine it. Once you feel fairly comfortable with your list, ask yourself, "What does this say about who I am?" Write your thoughts nonstop for as long as the ideas keep coming. Then look for new statements that have surfaced as the result of the exercise. Add them to your list. This is a process you may want to repeat two or three times a year.

Exercise INTO THE LOOKING GLASS

Place a mirror beside a phone that you use regularly. You will be surprised and immediately rewarded by what you learn. Watching yourself on the phone is a safe arena in which to study your body language. Here are some questions to ask yourself:

- How do you come across to others when you are comfortable? When you are uncomfortable?

- Does your body language match your words? Does it say you are comfortable with yourself? Will it make others comfortable with you?

Steffie found that seeing herself on videotape was even more instructive. She says, "I recommend using this method if it is available to you. It will teach you more about yourself in five minutes than hours of study using any other method. This was certainly true for me. In every test for assertiveness I have taken, I score in the ninety-ninth percentile. Yet I had no idea how my assertiveness looked to others until I saw a videotape of a committee meeting I attended. To my astonishment, I looked as though I had six-shooters for hands! I was pointing all the time, especially when I felt strongly about something, often reaching halfway across the table. People sitting next to me appeared to be in danger of having holes poked in their chests.

"For the next few months, I sat on my hands at meetings, until I broke myself of the habit of pointing. I also learned to sit back in my chair instead of looking like a lioness about to pounce. No one had to tell me this: The video said it all."

Exercise JOURNAL KEEPING

Start a journal, a private notebook strictly for you. Experiment with writing materials, and try different sizes of paper or notebooks to see what you are most comfortable with. Fill your journal with whatever you like—writing, drawings, cartoons, clippings, photos, anything that enhances the completeness and clarity of your thoughts and feelings.

Set aside a period of time to write in your journal on a regular basis. During that time, write without taking your pen off the paper for ten minutes or until you have exhausted your thoughts for the moment. Write in the first person, about whatever comes to mind; don't censor or edit your thoughts as you go along.

Date each entry so you can review your progress. Don't be concerned with spelling, grammar, or form.

While journal writing isn't for everyone, it is very likely that your journal will quickly become a trusted, supportive friend. Some people write regularly and some write only when they need to sort out a particular issue.

Exercise   *USING SELF-ASSESSMENT TOOLS*

In order to learn more about your behavioral style and nature, take the Myers-Briggs Type Indicator™. Consult a psychologist or someone else who is certified to administer the assessment, or you can use the book *LifeTYPES,* by Sandra Hirsch and Jean Kummerow, Ph.D. (1989). The Myers-Briggs Type Indicator is a valuable resource for understanding normal individual differences in personality. This assessment of sixteen types identifies the ways in which people can be different from each other and still be whole, healthy individuals who simply approach life differently.

Or read *Goddesses in Everywoman* (1984) or *Gods in Everyman* (1989) by Jean Shinoda Bolen, M.D. The author uses Greek mythology to present archetypes, or universal models, of masculine and feminine perspectives at their best or worst. These gods and goddesses represent clusters of values and traits. Learning about them can help you identify your own values and explain events and transitions in your life. Both of these approaches to making sense out of your behavior will help you develop compassion and understanding for yourself and others.

Exercise   *FANTASY CHOICES*

Consider each action below and decide whether you would make that choice or not—and *why*. If you had the time required, would you:

- Chair a reelection campaign for a good friend who is running for the school board?
- Accept a promotion to the next level in your business?

- Start your own business?

- Have another child, or parent a foster child, or become a Big Sister to a disadvantaged girl?

- Travel to Nepal and spend a month in a spiritual retreat in a monastery?

- Spend a week in solitude in the mountains or by the shore?

- Write a book?

- Chair a committee?

- Negotiate a contract by yourself?

What do your answers tell you about yourself?

Exercise   *TESTING YOUR METTLE*

Explore how different aspects of yourself are called upon in different life situations. In each of the following circumstances, jot down what skills, values, interests, talents, and experiences you would use:

- You are taking a road trip across the country with your best friend.

- You are asked to serve on a nonprofit board of directors.

- You are going on a blind date.

- You are counseling your college-aged child about making a career choice.

- You are having a job interview for your ideal job.

- You are opening a child care center in your home.

- You decide to learn to ski.

- You orchestrate the first-ever reunion of far-flung family members.

Exercise   *USING OTHERS AS MIRRORS*

To achieve congruence between your self-perception and the perception that others have about you requires working with others.

Of course, you must go beyond merely seeking confirmation of your own opinions about yourself. You must also be open to the input from others and not defensive. The goal is to see how others see you. Here are some simple ways to get feedback:

- Ask people who know you to describe you in three adjectives or phrases. They might say something like this: "I see you as a person who is thoughtful, who is committed to her work, and who takes pride in her family."

- Then ask them who you are *not*. Steffie's son said to her, "Mom, you're not someone who would abandon me when I needed you. You can't spell, and you don't deal well with boredom." Her husband's response was, "You aren't a wimp, unreasonable, or selfish." Sometimes it really pays to ask! A fellow worker told her, "You aren't always on time, detail-oriented, or easy to get around."

- Take your "I Am/I Am Not" list and share it with a few friends whose judgment you trust. Ask for their reactions. Don't pick people who will only want to please you or whom you can easily influence. Remember, you are looking for useful information.

Knowing yourself and acting on that self-knowledge form the foundation for becoming an empowered woman with a harmonious life. Being authentic ensures that you are open to learning, that you are serious about strengthening yourself, and that you are taking steps to fulfill your potential.

5

Risk Taking:

USING YOUR KNOWLEDGE, EXPERIENCE, AND COMPETENCE

//*Everything is sweetened by risk.***//**

—**Alexander Smith**

//*I do not think I will ever reach a stage when I will say, 'This is what I believe. Finished.' What I believe is 'alive . . . and open to growth.***//**

—**Madeleine L'Engle**

//*Woman must not accept; she must challenge. She must not be awed by that which has been built up around her; she must reverence that woman in her which struggles for expression.***//**

—**Margaret Sanger**

S HORTLY AFTER I WAS APPOINTED TO THE BOARD of directors of a hospital, I volunteered to chair the ethics committee. Some typical questions addressed by this group were: Does a person have the right to pull the plug on a life support system if he or she wishes to die? What should happen to frozen embryos when the couple who produced them as a backup in case their fertility program didn't work no longer need them—or if they divorce? How far do you go to save a human life when the quality of that life is being sacrificed?

One of my stated goals when I became chair of the committee was to ensure that the feminine perspective was incorporated into the policies of the hospital. This goal was soon put to the test.

A case was brought before us involving a thirty-five-year-old woman in the hospital who had lost her mental awareness as the unexpected complication of a chronic disease. She had no control over her mind, and the medical experts were certain she would never retrieve it. However, available treatment could keep her alive awhile longer.

The primary concern of the medical staff in this case was the legal considerations, and much circuitous discussion took place involving the woman's odds of living a long time if various treatments were applied or discontinued. The discussion was getting nowhere. It occurred to me that no one had mentioned the woman's family or relationships. Although I was the new kid on the block, I ventured to point out that the woman was more than a piece of flesh—she had a life. As I could see from a feminine point of view, she had relationships. Did she have a husband? How did *he* feel about her options? The whole chemistry of the meeting changed with the addition of a fresh perspective.

It turned out that the woman had been married only a few months and her husband had very high hopes that she would recover with treatment. This was the beginning of their marriage, and he couldn't possibly see it as the end of her life. He had expectations for their life together and needed time to come to terms with the way things actually were. Given this information, we decided to let the issue sit for a couple of months and then check back with the husband about his desires. After a short time had elapsed, the man came to see the situation as futile and asked that the treatment be discontinued; the woman died.

At that meeting of the ethics committee, I had to put my knowledge of the feminine perspective at risk. The stakes were high; as a new committee member, I could have lost credibility with the other members if my ideas were rejected. I was scared about exposing myself so soon and so fully. But it worked.

—Steffie

RISK TAKING AS A LIFE'S WORK

Taking risks involves understanding that we're constantly growing, shedding old ideas that don't work, learning, and moving on. It requires us to add new skills and education to adapt to a changing world. It means exposing ourselves to new experiences that are in alignment with our life's purpose or that have intrinsic interest for us alone.

Making use of your knowledge, experiences, and competence means doing things that keep you "fit"—physically, emotionally, intellectually, and spiritually. Physical fitness entails keeping your body healthy so it can serve you as you journey through life's adventures. Emotional fitness includes cultivating relationships that are nurturing and honest. Two or three friends (who may be family members) with whom you have a loving, caring relationship can fill this need. Intellectual fitness involves keeping informed about the issues surrounding your purpose or mission in life. You can't know it all, but you *can* become an expert in the thing you care most about. Read and discuss with experts those issues dear to your heart. Then share your knowledge through talking or doing. Maintaining spiritual fitness can be achieved in many ways—by taking a week off by yourself, spending an hour a day to meditate or contemplate life, or reading inspiring works of great beings that "fill you up" and nurture you spiritually.

Risk taking also includes putting ourselves at risk in our relationships—both personal and professional. With a feminine focus on connection, this can be uncomfortable. Yet there are times when we need to challenge the boss, say no to the kids, give a gift to someone even though we fear it may be rejected, or say yes to a relationship even though the last one ended in disaster.

Payoffs for Risk Taking

▶ Your self-confidence grows as you become willing to take greater risks.

▶ You gain respect from others as someone who stands her ground and knows what she is talking about.

▶ You attract others with the same interests, vision, and competencies; this allows you to pool your strengths and create power in numbers.

▶ You become a desirable member of powerful groups, which will extend your influence even further.

A Life on the Edge of the New

Lenore Walker is a renowned expert on domestic violence, but she didn't begin that way. In the mid 1970s, she was intrigued by the issue of women in abusive relationships. After six years as a psychologist, she applied for and received a grant to research the issue. As the result of her research, she published a book (*The Battered Woman*, 1979), which, to her total surprise, became a best-seller and the leading treatise on the subject. "If I had known where that book would go," she now says, "I would have been terrified."

Quickly, her credibility fueled by the book's reception, Lenore began to lecture on domestic violence. This exposed her to more information, which in turn allowed her to put out more information. Her competence in the subject grew. She became aware that the laws governing the area were designed for men fighting men as equal opponents, not at all the case for women in battering situations. Her charge became clear: to prove that this assumption base was not applicable to domestic violence cases. Lenore earned her doctoral degree, learned about law, and wrote more books, including the popular work, *Terrifying Love: Why Battered Women Kill and How Society Responds* (1989). She became a sought-after public speaker and appeared on "The Oprah Winfrey Show."

She was asked to be an expert witness, helping women to be considered differently from men when they picked up a weapon in self-defense or when in despera-tion, following years of beatings, they hired someone else to protect them. She also worked to seek pardons for women, imprisoned under previous laws, who had been in life-threatening situations and had struck back to save their lives.

Lenore gained knowledge and took risks to communicate that knowledge in high-exposure situations— courtrooms and lecture halls—before hundreds of people. Her path consisted of a long process of contemplation, commitment, conviction, and courage. At times, she had to become verbally aggressive (which was not her normal style) in order to achieve her ends. She learned that cooperation was only one tool among many and that she didn't need to cooperate just for cooperation's sake.

Think of all that Lenore accomplished through risk taking. One person who was interested in domestic violence now has a worldwide reputation as an expert in this pioneering field. Her ability to change the options available to battered women has been magnified a hundredfold.

TOOLS OF EMPOWERMENT

Exercise *LAYERING YOUR COMPETENCE*

Find out what you need to become competent, whether your field of interest is professional or personal. Start off with what you need to know—perhaps a degree, or certain skills—and then put that knowledge at risk. The process is much like that of a nautilus adding chambers to its shell. You learn a skill, put it at risk, learn a new skill, and put that at risk, endlessly building upon your competence and upgrading your personal resources. Take Lenore Walker, for example. At first, she needed research and grant-writing skills. Later, she added to her repertoire knowledge of how to manage intellectual resources, write a book, present to large groups, testify in court, and lead. Note: You don't need to learn everything all at once, but only as needed!

The challenge is to swim out a little deeper each time without getting in over your head. Talk to people who have done what you're contemplating and find out what the measures of success for that endeavor are. Then you can evaluate whether or not you're up to the task. Often, you will know intuitively if you should say yes or no. Steffie recalls, "Once I was asked to speak to the Young Presidents Organization—a group for individuals who are presidents of their companies and who each made five million dollars by the age of forty. The catch was that I was given twenty-four hours' notice! I declined. I regretted being unprepared for that type of performance, but I knew that I would do myself more harm than good by accepting at the time."

Exercise *THE CONSTRUCTIVE CRITIC*

The kind of self-assessment we do as a part of taking risks needs to include self-criticism—*constructive* self-criticism. To take your own and others' criticism to heart without first viewing it with a discriminating eye is useless at best and damaging to your self-esteem at worst. It's essential to evaluate the nature and quality of the critic, whether it's your friend or yourself talking. The punitive or overly restrictive critic claims to have high standards (so we listen!), but actually has dumb, unattainable, or even cruel standards. On the other hand, the constructive critic listens to and makes use of the voices of both your positive and negative critics and uses reasonable, fair, and reachable standards.

The following exercise brings out and develops the constructive critic. It is derived from the work of Peter G. Ossorio, Ph.D. Pick an incident in your life or something about yourself you are particularly critical of (or you can pick a quality others are critical of). First make a diagnosis. Ask yourself, "What's wrong here?"

1. Consult the *negative critic*. List all the things you think you've done wrong, or that are wrong with you. Then step back and look at the list as if you were an objective third party. Cross out the points that are ridiculous, exaggerated, or inaccurate. You can ask a trusted friend to do the same. Acknowledge the truth and usefulness of the remaining criticisms and thank the negative critic for her input. Send her out for a well-deserved break.

2. Consult the *positive critic*. Notice what you have done that is right. In particular, pay attention to the following elements. Check whether what you've done was:

   ▪ Appropriate, given the situation

   ▪ Ethically correct

   ▪ In your best interest

   ▪ Fun

   Add anything else that seems positive about yourself or your behavior. Then come up with a prescription for change. Ask yourself, "How can I make it better?"

3. With the above information in hand, ask yourself, "How could things be improved?" List all the possible ways that come to mind. Don't censor yourself.

4. Check the prescriptions. Ask yourself, "Will this help keep me out of trouble (or at least keep me from going terribly wrong)?" Note that this is different from "Is it guaranteed to work?" or "Is it the perfect solution?" or "Will I ever regret it?" or "Will it solve everything?" These are perfectionist standards, which are impossible to meet, whereas

checking to see if the prescription is headed in the right direction is a reasonable standard.

5. Finally, look at the prescriptions for improving things and see how you can put some or all of them into action. You might want to prioritize them. Set a time to take the first step. Put it in your appointment book.

Use this exercise any time you find you are putting the screws to yourself, and get the constructive critic to work!

Exercise   *SIZING YOURSELF UP*

Write a résumé highlighting your skills and talents. Focus on what you know how to do that someone else would be willing to pay for. Then ask two or three people who have worked with you and know your assets to evaluate your self-assessment. If possible, include one hard-nosed man. He will probably be more objective about both your strengths and weaknesses than you can be. (We women often tend to underestimate our abilities. And women as "critics" can be too "nice" to avoid hurting others' feelings.)

Once you have your revised résumé in hand, look for the areas of weakness. Ask yourself what you need to do to achieve your goals. Your game plan may include everything from learning how to dress appropriately for the situation to acquiring specific technical knowledge. You may decide that you need to join certain associations, gain experience in a related field, eliminate an annoying speech pattern, or enhance your sense of humor.

Next, take action. Figure out some good risks you could take and train to meet those risks. Practice presenting your expertise. Exposing your strengths and competencies will only enhance your confidence in your abilities and allow you to take bigger and bigger risks. Also, clarify for yourself what you are and are not willing to risk. Is it family? Physical safety? Peer approval? While some people are willing to risk all, you may not want to or have to.

Exercise   *PUTTING YOUR RISKS*
IN PERSPECTIVE

Allow yourself some time to think about what risks you easily take today that you couldn't take a year ago—or five years ago. Cite specific examples to prove it to yourself. As you go through this process, think of yourself as a vessel that grows larger and larger as you learn to accommodate more of life. Perhaps you can now handle speaking to a group of five hundred people, when before you would tremble at the thought of speaking to five. Maybe you've become more versatile in your communication, growing comfortable with writing as well as speaking. These are the sorts of things you need to track in order to feel confident about taking new risks and moving forward in your life.

It has been said that "change is inevitable; growth is optional." Being able to take reasonable risks is an acknowledgment of the value of lifelong learning, and a commitment to an ongoing discovery of who you truly are.

6

Vision:

SEEING WHAT IS
AND WHAT COULD BE

//When I look into the future, it's so bright it burns my eyes.**//**

—**Oprah Winfrey**

//Idealists . . . foolish enough to throw caution to the winds . . . have advanced mankind and have enriched the world.**//**

—**Emma Goldman**

//I began to have an idea of my life, not as the slow shaping of achievement to fit my preconceived purposes, but as the gradual discovery and growth of a purpose which I did not know.**//**

—**Joanna Field**

ONE AFTERNOON WHEN I WAS ELEVEN, I went to visit my grandmother. We sat together on her porch, a spacious, screened-in sanctuary high above a valley lined with fragrant fir trees. Somehow, this frail, elegant lady with a halo of wild, white hair managed, by her self-possessed manner, to make me feel good. I always looked forward to the times when I could see her. She served us lemonade in big glasses with fat red, yellow, and green stripes on them. From our perch we could look down the valley and see the mountains turning from green to blue to lavender in the distance. Blue jays fluttered past on their way to the bird feeder. Though I was just a kid, I recognized that this spot was a glorious place of solitude and peace.

I asked her what she liked to do out there on her porch. "I think about my vision," she said. For a long time, I sat thinking about her answer. The only person I had ever heard about who had a vision was Joan of Arc. Finally, I dared to ask her, "What is your vision about?" She turned her gaze from the valley to me and said, "It's about what could be."

Twenty years later, I understood what she meant. Forty years later, I recognized how lucky I was to have had someone in my life at an early age who invited me to think about what could be, and who showed me, by her example, that doing so was something that mattered.

—Steffie

A "HOLY CAUSE"

Vision, more than any other characteristic, sets the empowered woman apart from others. Anyone is capable of being visionary. In life, a vision may become clear at any stage or age. However, visions most frequently emerge in midlife, once you have come to see that the true power lies within you, not in the external symbols of success. A vision arises from a need to feed the soul, a spiritual crisis of sorts. Often, a personal connection with a higher power fuels and sustains the vision.

Artists typically understand this connection with a higher power. They realize that their inspiration comes from inside them, yet is directed by a muse who is using them as a channel for creative expression. It is as if little vision seeds have been strewn throughout the world. When they take hold within you, it may seem as though you are being directed by a mysterious force that is acting *through* you.

THE POWER AND THE GLORY OF VISION

Vision is a serious matter. It is the guiding light that brings direction to your life. Although it is rooted in the present reality, it is also a catalyst that brings about a new, bigger reality. A vision is not a dream, and it's vastly larger than most goals. It's something in which you would willingly invest your whole being.

Visionaries believe that they can shape the future. This is a significant point. Rather than holding to a fatalistic notion that the future will just happen in a way that is outside of their control, they believe the future can be influenced in the direction of what they see as possible today.

Articulating a vision takes courage. As you express your vision, you may be struck with an uncomfortable feeling of being grandiose or self-important. You may ask yourself, "Who do I think I am to have such a vision?" I think this happens because we are not in the habit of stepping outside ourselves to contemplate something bigger than ourselves. But vision is the work of the human spirit; thus it is about things that matter to humanity. Visions *do* sound lofty— because they are. They ask you to live your life for some higher purpose that is deeply meaningful to you.

PEBBLES AND EPIPHANIES

A vision may grow out of the things that cause you discomfort, those complaints and concerns that stay with you over time, like a pebble in your shoe. We might say that your vision arises from the "pebble" in your soul—the aspects of life that, year after year, continue to annoy or even anger you. Discontent may give rise to a vision.

Of course, not all visions spring from anger or indignation. Sometimes they are born from a positive experience or from the possibilities and potential inherent in situations and people. Specific life occurrences, both tragic and euphoric, may trigger the birth of a vision, or it may be created from many small events. What is most important is that you listen to your inner voice as it expresses to you the things you really care about.

"When I applied to graduate school I had to write an essay on why I wanted to become a psychologist," says Carolyn. "I knew exactly what the answer was and I remember sitting down and writing it out quickly.

"I had spent my entire college career as managing editor of one publication or another. In that role, it was my job to see that everyone got their work done to meet the deadlines. I loved the challenge of finding ways of working with people to bring out the best they had to offer. This seminal experience inspired me to keep looking for ways to participate in creating a world where people discover their inner strengths and live them out in their everyday lives. In my life, activities toward this end have taken many forms—being a mother, practicing psychotherapy, teaching meditation, training graduate students, and writing articles on the expression of spirituality in daily life. This idea of bringing out the best in people is a recurring theme, and one that gives me a great deal of satisfaction.

"My seeds of discontent, then, come from the situations in which I find myself or others not living out this greatness; these situations spur me to regain my focus and get back on track."

VISION AND GENDER

Both men and women have visions. Nevertheless, throughout history, men have had more freedom to express their visions than women. Few can deny that America's founding fathers had a magnificent vision. But men's visions are often different from women's, because they spring from a different perspective on life, as we discussed in Chapter Three. For example, the male concept of law is founded on the creation of an orderly society in support of the protection of individual rights (in other words, a masculine perspective). It doesn't effectively address conflicting responsibilities or conflicting relationships (child custody disputes, for example), which are central to the feminine perspective. Likewise, men have traditionally been the promoters, inventors, and carriers of technology but at times they have not dealt with the consequences of their discoveries. Quite the opposite: They often tried to claim responsibility for the consequences and failed. A much-publicized example of this involves Robert Oppenheimer, the physicist who assisted in the development of the atomic bomb. Later, stricken by conscience, Oppenheimer tried to convince his fellow scientists that they were wrong to continue working on the bomb, but he and those who agreed with him were discredited and overruled.

Warren Ziegler has trained fifteen thousand people in the envisioning process over the last twenty years. He works with all types of business, nonprofit, and religious organizations to create visions that transform their particular community. He says that although both men and women are striving toward "social justice in a sustainable world," he finds differences in the form and tone of their visions (Ziegler, personal conversation, 1992). Men's visions have more to do with bringing about change through transformation of societal structures and institutions. They also focus more on ideas and practical solutions, and they tend to use cognitive language. Women's visions, on the other hand, typically concentrate on bringing about transformation through changes in human relationships, and through bonding and community. Women emphasize feelings and use what Ziegler calls "a more flowing vocabulary of intimacy." He says that women are more willing to consider true transformation, that is, to bring into existence something that has never existed before. (As the bearers of children, it seems logical that women are necessarily the carriers of hope!)

At this point in history, Ziegler also finds that women are "unquestionably the best facilitators and envisioners." Finally, when men and women practice envisioning in partnership, they have a powerful impact on each other, as they move beyond their original approaches to incorporate each others' ways.

Payoffs for Vision

▶ **You have a sense of purpose on the good days and the bad, a reason to go on.**

▶ **You have a focus around which to build your life.**

▶ **You have a sense of your own character and uniqueness.**

▶ **You invite a greater number of people into your life.**

▶ **You bring spirituality into your work.**

▶ **It is more compelling and worthwhile to take risks.**

Vision Shapes a Life

The life of Elise Boulding exemplifies an evolving, yet overriding, vision. Ultimately nominated for the Nobel Peace Prize, Elise began her lifelong quest for peace at a very young age. Her first significant step toward formulating her vision occurred in her teens, when she became a member of the Society of Friends, a religious community dedicated to peace.

Elise believed that peace begins at home. With her husband, noted economist

Kenneth Boulding, she raised five children, working hard to resolve value conflicts and to foster cooperation within her family and community. She began her second career at the age of forty-eight, learning skills to further support her vision. She earned a doctorate in sociology, taught at the University of Colorado, and later chaired the sociology department at Dartmouth College.

Elise went on to work internationally on problems of peace and world order as both a scholar and an activist. She served as a member of the U.S. Commission for UNESCO (the United Nations Educational, Scientific, and Cultural Organization), the international jury of the UNESCO Prize for Peace Education, and the governing board of the United Nations University. In the mid sixties, she helped found the International Peace Research Association. Some of this organization's work has been incorporated into the policies and initiatives of the United Nations. During that tumultuous time, she routinely put herself at risk by lobbying and participating in peace demonstrations. Elise continues to spread her vision as an author and lecturer and has greatly influenced the study of peace.

Elise's vision took her beyond the assumption that peace is simply the absence of war to an understanding of peace as a perspective and a set of skills that emerge from training and responsible action. Her life also shows that sometimes we need to cast about for the best way to manifest our vision. Elise didn't always win. In fact, she lost the one time she ran for political office, during the Vietnam War. Instead of politics, she found an arena more suited to her talents and one in which she could address her concerns throughout her life—the academic world. In this way she was able to extend her ideas about peace and global civilization to many others for generations to come.

Now in her seventies, Elise is tall and slightly stooped, with a stance and manner evocative of the women who won the West. Strong and centered, she calls forth the best in those she meets. She is as stimulating and enriching as she is comfortable to be around. One cannot spend time with her without sensing how much her life has been dedicated to the pursuit of her vision. You feel grateful to know her, to hear her present her research and her creative thoughts, to be challenged by her wisdom, and to be touched by her smile.

TOOLS OF EMPOWERMENT

Naturally, most of us have not had training in visioning, any more than we have had classes on using intuition. Yet visioning is part of our human makeup. How do you uncover your vision and put it to work? Quite simply, by invitation. You cannot analyze your vision into being. It needs to come from your heart, not your head, and bringing it forth requires solitude and introspection. You can begin the process of defining your vision using these three steps. They are based on Warren Ziegler's work. (See his book, *A Mindbook of Exercises for Futures-Inventors*, 1982.)

Exercise   *STEP ONE: FINDING THE SOURCE*

Visions may emerge from discontent (the desire to change something you feel is negative) or from inspiration (a sense of excitement or wonder).

The Impetus of Anger

Take half an hour to write down the things that bother you, on a local, as well as a global, scale. Dump out everything you can think of. When you have this pile of "pebbles" before you, go back through it and look for these things:

- Recurring themes under which to group the items on your list that offend your sense of justice or morality

- The items that trigger the most profound feelings of anger or dismay

- Changes that you passionately want to occur in the world, especially those you have thought about for some time

As you do this exercise, you may uncover more than one source of discontent. Isolating your vision sometimes involves a process of elimination in which you define your issue in comparison to someone else's. Also, check for deeper issues; there may be one unifying theme underlying your two or three most compelling areas of discontent.

Retrieving Inspiration

Some people have the experience of a vision coming to them full-blown and unbidden and staying with them throughout their lives. More often we discount or forget these experiences; however, through contemplation, we can uncover the memories of these visionary experiences.

Think back on times in your life when you were inspired and excited about the possibilities in the world. In each of these instances, the memory is vivid and clear, and you recall distinctly what made the moment so significant to you. When you think back on it, there's an "Aha!" quality to the experience, a sense that *this is how life really is and how it could be all the time.* It's strongly felt. There is no denying the power of that experience for you, even though it may have meant nothing to someone else who was present. This path of reflection can also reveal your vision.

Exercise   ## STEP TWO:
SHARING YOUR VISION

Speaking your vision aloud to someone who will just listen gives it reality and substance. This may be hard to believe, but the best listener is someone you don't know well, or even at all! What you want is a person who has no vested interest in your vision, and no intention of "helping" you figure it out. If you do use a friend, make sure that person meets these criteria.

Deep Listening

Once you have found your listener, tell the individual that you need him or her to listen "deeply." Explain that deep listening is different from "active listening," in which the listener nods his or her head, utters words of encouragement, and helps to move your thoughts along with supportive comments. In contrast, deep listening is the art of emptying oneself of *one's own* thoughts and feelings in order to receive the speaker's message nonjudgmentally. The listener's objective is to understand the speaker on both a content and a feeling level. (The most adept listeners may even be able to pick up a third level—the unspoken "essence" of what you are saying.)

After you have established these ground rules, proceed in the following manner. Both of you need to get comfortable. You want the listener to remain silent for at least five minutes while you articulate your vision. It would be best for the listener not to look at you at all. It is helpful to sit next to each other but facing opposite directions. While the other person is listening, you are talking. As you begin this exercise, it may seem as if you are talking to yourself. That is exactly what you want, for you are having an important discussion with yourself about the core meaning of your life.

After you have talked for five to ten minutes, have the listener ask any questions he or she has about what you mean. This will help clarify your thoughts as well. Then ask the listener to repeat your vision back to you. Work to refine it until it pleases you. At that point, write it down.

Here are some examples of visions:

- Anita Roddick is president of The Body Shop, an international body care products company with a social and environmental conscience. She has a vision of a world in which you don't have to lose your soul to succeed in business. She says, "There is a better way. You can rewrite the book on business. You can trade ethically, be committed to social and global responsibility. You can empower your employees. It is okay to have fun" (Roddick, 1991, p. 249). The company uses refillable containers. It also campaigns against animal testing for cosmetics and uses natural ingredients for its products. All employees do community work and Roddick has involved the corporation in a range of environmental causes from saving the rain forests to recycling the containers for the cosmetics she sells.

- Early pioneer women had a vision of civilizing the country and preserving the culture they were leaving behind. They tucked iris bulbs, musical instruments, and books—the seeds of little visions—into their packed covered wagons.

- Elise Boulding envisioned a world without weapons.

The following are examples of the visions of some women from our workshops, aged twenty-five to sixty, most of whom have a high school education or some college. They represent a diversity of backgrounds, marital status, and socioeconomic situations. Most are first-line managers in large corporations. We asked them to complete the following sentence: "I envision a world where . . ." Here are some of their responses:

- Children are able to realize their full potential.
- Diversity is recognized, respected, and taught in the school system.
- People grow old with dignity.
- There is equal tax treatment for all.
- There is no hunger.
- Lesbians and gays are accepted as valued people.
- People can live and work without being in conflict with their values.
- All people have a home to live in.
- There is no child abuse or neglect.
- People live in harmony with each other and the earth.

Exercise   STEP THREE: REALITY CHECK

There are true visions and false visions. Warren Ziegler (1982) has identified these marks of a true vision:

- True visions are concrete and specific.
- True visions do not dissolve.
- True visions are "owned" by their visionary.
- True visions are not violent.

Write your vision in one sentence. Make it brief and to the point. Run it by people. Do they nod their heads and understand? Ask yourself:

- Is your vision concrete and specific? Can it serve as a basis for taking action?
- Does your vision stay with you? Is it compelling? If you have forgotten it in two weeks, two months, or even two years, clearly it is not the core meaning of your life.

- Do you feel energized talking about it? Is it really a reflection of you? Although you may feel shy or uncomfortable at first, in time expressing your vision should feel as natural to you as breathing.

- Is your vision nonviolent? The nonviolent aspect of true visions is what distinguishes the Martin Luther Kings and the Elise Bouldings from the Hitlers and Saddam Husseins of the world (or, among the ranks of female tyrants, from a person like Catherine de Médicis, queen of France, who, to preserve power, murdered her opponents without remorse). At times, violence may ensue from a vision, but it cannot *be* the vision. King's vision was about equal rights, to which certain people reacted violently. Hitler's vision was about a supreme race, forcibly served by others. By definition, Hitler's vision was violent and, therefore, false.

Spend some time during the next few weeks testing out your vision against these criteria.

Exercise *MAKING IT HAPPEN*

When you have come up with a clear statement of your vision, one that "fits," follow these steps:

1. Write it down someplace where you will see it constantly so that it can become part of your mindset.

2. Imagine exactly what the world would look like if your vision were a reality. What would the public institutions such as courts and schools be like? How would people behave toward one another at work and in families? What would the physical environment (cities, homes, workplaces, the outdoors) be like? Would life be any different for teens, children, the elderly? In what ways?

3. Brainstorm ideas about how these imaginings could be brought into reality. What role—direct or indirect—could you play? Think of a specific arena where you could start making your vision happen.

4. Set a goal to begin bringing that vision into reality. It might be a tiny little first step toward manifesting it in your own life, or a larger goal that might involve a community

project—whatever suits you *right now*. Lay out a plan of action for carrying it out and set a specific time to take the first step. (See the section on setting goals in Chapter Eleven.)

Persistence Pays

If pursuing your vision isn't working, it doesn't necessarily mean that the vision is wrong (although you may want to revisit the envisioning process). It may mean that the way you are trying to accomplish it is wrong, or it may need to be played out on a smaller scale in your personal life. To change the world, we have to start with our own behavior and our own lives. All the "little" things we do are as essential to carrying out our vision as are any "big" projects.

A vision needs to be backed up with hard work, common sense, risk taking, and a sense of timing. The nice thing about a vision is that it doesn't have to get crumpled even when you fall flat on your face. Get up, evaluate what isn't working, refine your methods, and correct them.

Finding Your Anchor

One problem with not having your own vision is that you can be pulled into living out someone else's. If you have your own, you can share activities with others who have similar or complementary visions without being swept up in a life or actions that do not bring you a sense of being true to yourself. That is why your vision, in addition to being your guiding light, is also your anchor. It reveals and ties you to what is most important to you. It allows you to determine your goals and values and to bring the highest meaning to your life.

Focusing on your vision lifts you out of the mundane sameness of everyday life. It reminds you of your higher purpose for living and expands and enlivens your spirit.

7

Health:

USING YOUR
ENERGY WISELY

❏❏ *The trouble with the rat race is that even if you win you're still a rat.* **❏❏**
—**Lily Tomlin**

❏❏ *Women's work is always toward wholeness.* **❏❏**
—**May Sarton**

❏❏ *However broken down is the spirit's shrine, the spirit is there all the same.* **❏❏**
—**Nigerian proverb**

WHEN I LEARNED THAT MY DAUGHTER HAD been in a serious car accident, I immediately flew to California to be with her. She was badly injured and I didn't want to take my eyes off her. Yet at the time, I was ill with bronchitis, on my second antibiotic prescription (the first hadn't worked), and fearful that the infection would deteriorate into pneumonia. Given all this, I sized up my situation to see what I needed to do.

First, I decided to let other people support me (*not* easy for me!). I made arrangements to stay with a friend who was very willing to take care of me. She fed me, did my laundry, and listened to my concerns. I also established rules for myself to preserve my energy. For example, I forced myself to leave the hospital at a certain time each day, turning bedside duty over to Amy's friends. To guard my own health, I made myself sleep at least six hours a night. When I woke up, I meditated for an hour, took a relaxing shower, had a leisurely breakfast, and went for a short walk.

I trusted that I didn't have to be at the hospital every minute (something I couldn't have done fifteen years ago—I'd have been afraid not to be there). I took breaks throughout the day to rest or walk. And I changed the rules I had made when I needed to. Exhausted from being on my feet during the day shift, I switched to the night shift, asking a nurse to find me a cot so I could sleep at my daughter's side.

This ability to take care of myself while caring for another was hard-won. Since childhood, I have been frequently sick. Because of this, I developed a fantasy idea of health. Although I dreamed of being healthy, I saw it as a transitory and fickle state of perfect, absolutely unblemished physical well-being. Later on, when I had a period of years during which I actually was illness-free, I figured that being healthy meant I could do anything, so I pushed my body too hard and created more health problems for myself. Then I went through a phase of resignation, thinking, "Well, I'm going to get sick anyway, so I might as well drive myself until I do." Finally, I came to a point where I could allow myself to be sick occasionally without panicking or feeling guilty. I realized that I could indeed take some steps to monitor and maintain my health.

The best way I can think of to describe my change of attitude is that I eventually established a friendly relationship with my body rather than demanding that it support me— or being angry when it did not. In Eastern spiritual traditions, it is said that God dwells within us as our inner spirit and that the body is a temple for this in-dwelling divinity. Seeing my body in this way made me realize that I have good reason to take care of it: To nourish my soul, I have to nurture the body that gives it a place on this earth! This understanding was fundamental to changing my attitude toward my body. I came to see it as a friendly companion helping me along on my journey through life. I now feel appreciative and nurturing toward it, while acknowledging that I still don't have the reserves of strength and energy that others do and maybe never will.

—Carolyn

THE MYTH OF PERFECT HEALTH

One fallacy many women have bought into is the belief that if we do things right we will never be sick or upset and we will always get everything done that needs to be done. This is an insidious side effect of the "Superwoman Syndrome."

In reality, being healthy doesn't mean *always* being well and sane, nor, in opposite terms, does it mean *never* being sick or crazy. Instead, it involves learning to care for yourself so you are sick less often and, even when you are sick, you have the emotional and physical reserves to heal.

Pacing yourself is a key part of health. By guarding your energy, you can protect yourself against serious problems, so you are less likely to get sick or "come unglued." Guarding yourself also means stopping when you need to stop.

PITFALLS TO PONDER

One of women's pitfalls is to identify ourselves too strongly with our bodies. It is important to realize that you are more than your body. In the past, when people asked me how I was, I answered based on my physical state. "I'm terrible," I would say. "I have pneumonia." Gradually, I learned not to identify with my body, but instead to identify with my inner self (my spirit or inner being), which is not affected by illness or other circumstances of life. This freed me to be happy—even ecstatic—during times when I was extremely ill. There were times when I was sick but still felt very good about some activity in my life, such as learning something new that excited me. I began to pay attention to "how I was" in other than physical ways.

My daughter exemplified this in a very inspirational way following her accident. I was struck by the fact that she did not equate her physical state with her spiritual well-being. Visitors, too, were stunned when they walked into her room and glimpsed her cut and disfigured face, her broken limbs in traction—and then heard her say, "I'm great!" as a radiant light shone from her face.

Another pitfall for women is to ask too much of ourselves, especially emotionally. While women are better than men about getting medical treatment for physical ailments, we often do not try to find a health care practitioner or psychotherapist whom we like and who will understand us. Women should feel comfortable interviewing prospective medical practitioners and therapists and examining their background, credentials, and experience in dealing with the issues we are wrestling with.

Women are better at asking for psychological help (probably outnumbering men in psychotherapy four to one); nonetheless, we frequently won't seek therapy if our partners don't accompany us or if they disapprove. We need to give ourselves permission to address our own needs; the problem may have nothing to do with our partner.

Yet another pitfall for women is that we tend to be poor delegators, both at home and at work. Sensitive to other people who need to be taken care of, we may feel we are the only ones who can help. Also, out of friendship or a need to assume the important role of caretaker, women sometimes take on other people's problems even if they are too big to handle or if someone else might be better equipped to solve them.

I know a nurse who always intervenes whenever anyone in her family is ill or has a problem. This loving, caring earth mother ended up seriously ill herself after spending two weeks at her father's bedside in the hospital. She felt it was her duty to be there whenever he asked for her and to take over all the nursing functions that the staff would allow. She slept in a chair at night and refused to go to the cafeteria for meals. Her distraught family couldn't persuade her to go home even to shower and change clothes. She kept going until she collapsed, and then there was no one to be at the hospital with her father. Her family had to take care of her as well as continuing to assume her responsibilities at home. While this is an extreme example, I have noticed that I, too, sometimes overextend myself in subtle ways until I am crushed by the cumulative burden and can't figure out why I am worn out!

Finally, women sometimes fail to weigh the wisdom of our own hearts and minds about what we need. We will listen to others rather than to our own intuition. We turn to experts, people we know in authority, or friends we trust.

I am reminded of the joke about a woman's New Year's resolutions. The first resolution was: "I won't get involved in other people's problems." The second was: "Wherever help is needed, I will be there." It shows what a strong and automatic response it is for us to ignore our own emotional needs while catering to everyone else.

The following passage from Anne Morrow Lindbergh's *Gift from the Sea* (1975, pp. 58–59) illustrates what women have to strive for. During a solitary vacation at the beach, the writer found a shell and took it home to remind her of the importance of solitude:

> Moon shell, who named you? Some intuitive woman I like to think. I shall give you another name—Island shell. I cannot live forever on my island. But I can take you back to my desk in Connecticut. You will sit there and fasten your single eye upon me. You will make me think, with your smooth circles winding inward to the

tiny core, of the island I lived on for a few weeks. You will say to me "solitude." You will remind me that I must try to be alone for part of each year, even a week or a few days; and for part of each day, even for an hour or a few minutes in order to keep my core, my center, my island-quality. You will remind me that unless I keep the island-quality intact somewhere within me, I will have little to give my husband, my children, my friends or the world at large. You will remind me that woman must be still as the axis of a wheel in the midst of her activities; that she must be the pioneer in achieving this stillness, not only for her own salvation, but for the salvation of family life, of society, perhaps even of our civilization.

A pitfall we don't want to borrow from men is the tendency men have to abuse themselves physically, injuring themselves in sports by competing with others and with their memories of themselves as younger men. They are also more likely than women to put off seeking medical attention; frequently, they wait for a crisis. Emotionally, they harm themselves by shutting down and chronically channeling all their feelings into anger.

Workaholism is an individual and cultural problem that affects both men and women. In many work cultures, working through lunch, working overtime, skipping vacation, or taking on ever-increasing responsibilities are de rigueur. This kind of behavior leads to what Anne Morrow Lindbergh has described by using the German word *Zerrissenheit,* or "torn-apartness," a sense of being scattered and having no direction—even to the extreme of complete physical collapse.

The Right to Respite

Sometimes you have to simply retreat from your obligations in moments of tremendous emotional strain. A friend and colleague, Marcia Lattanzi-Licht, is a nurse-counselor who has an international reputation as a speaker and trainer in hospice work. While serving as

Payoffs for Health

▶ Your physical condition is more stable, rather than being a roller coaster of peaks and valleys.

▶ You become a more responsible, reliable person.

▶ Having realistic expectations of your body and your emotional resources makes you happier and more in sync with yourself.

▶ Spending your energy wisely rather than diluting it allows you to maximize your life and achieve your goals.

▶ You have more joy in your life.

head of the bereavement team for a hospice, she was engaged in several major projects, including a training film for law enforcement officers about responding to sudden death, when her own teenaged daughter was killed by a drunken driver. When she came back to work she had to sort out which projects she could resume and which she had to drop until she was able to do them justice. Stricken by the blow of her own terrible loss, she just could not continue her work with bereaved families or her supervision of other hospice workers. She knew that if she didn't take care of herself first, she couldn't do competent work with others and would sink further into sorrow herself.

Marcia decided to keep working on the film, however, for an important reason. Her daughter Ellen had been enthusiastic about the project, and shortly before she was killed, she had said to her mother, "It's good that you're working with cops because they need all the help they can get!" The filming had been done before Ellen was killed and only the editing was left. Completing the film was a manageable task, one that could give her life meaning in her grief. Consequently Marcia finished this work and

dedicated it to Ellen as an   In time she was able to re-
expression of her love for her.   sume her other roles.

TOOLS OF EMPOWERMENT

Exercise   *SCALING BACK*

Realize that your energy is finite. Pick your battles and decide where investing your energy will give you the greatest reward. Do things that are aligned with your vision. And remember, if you don't have a vision, you will be buffeted by the needs of others and will end up skimping on your own.

Assess your physical and emotional strengths and weaknesses. Certain issues may set you off or trigger illness; be aware of what they are and look for patterns. Ask yourself, "When have I felt like this before?" Sometimes others are better able to see the patterns in our lives than we are. Our mother once pointed out to me that I got sick every Monday morning following a weekend during which my stepchildren were visiting. I then realized that I was killing myself to be a perfect stepmother and took pains to let up.

Once you are aware of your patterns, set clear limits for yourself and stick to them. In times of emotional turmoil, to determine whether you need to step out of your normal responsibilities or get back to them, spend some time alone meditating about the proper choice. Ask others to give you feedback about your emotional state. Often, family and friends have insights that can help you.

Exercise   *USING YOUR EMOTIONS WISELY*

Work on using your emotions appropriately. Emotions are very powerful if they are used wisely. Many women see themselves as having to be emotionless at work. This emotional suppression is bound to increase the likelihood that they will end up with traditionally "male" diseases, like heart attacks.

When Margaret Thatcher was prime minister of Great Britain, she gave a speech during a time when her soldier son had been missing in action for five days. The double burden of running a country and handling her own personal fears as a mother showed in her eyes, which filled with tears during her presentation. Those who watched her were touched by this genuine, utterly appropriate display of emotion.

Exercise   *SCHEDULING PLEASURE*

Take time to put your needs and wants up for review. Think about what you want to do for yourself alone, something that will bring you pleasure. Do an activity just for fun every day, perhaps one you enjoyed doing as a child. For example, I returned to a childhood hobby of sculpting whimsical creatures out of clay. This simple project takes little time and gives me enormous pleasure.

Take time to be alone. Many women feel guilty doing this or are rigid about what's acceptable (for example, they won't give up "career time" to do something fun and creative for themselves). They may feel selfish for not spending time in service to others. Music, art, dance, or creative engineering projects are all excellent ways to renew your physical and emotional energy. It is also energizing to change your routine. Take a bubble bath instead of a shower, or walk barefoot through the grass instead of using the sidewalk. Seize opportunities to have fun all by yourself.

The benefits of solitude cannot be overstated. Being alone allows you to reconnect with yourself, to contemplate life's puzzles, and to tap into your intuitive wisdom. It teaches you how to comfort and calm yourself. Often, it is a way to step back and establish some perspective on your life. Solitude revitalizes and refreshes you so that you can return to your daily life with renewed vigor and energy.

8

Humor:

APPROACHING LIFE
WITH A LIGHT HEART

▮▮ *He who laughs, lasts.* **▮▮**

—**Mary Pettibone Poole**

▮▮ *A person without a sense of humor is like a wagon without springs—jolted by every pebble in the road.* **▮▮**

—**Harriet Beecher Stowe**

▮▮ *We cannot really love anybody with whom we never laugh.* **▮▮**

—**Agnes Repplier**

93

I WAS STARING OUT THE WINDOW at the dandelions on our front lawn one spring day when I was feeling particularly overwhelmed by the demands of my chosen roles as wife, mother, and household manager. Never mind being upset about work; I couldn't even *think* about work. It was the story everyone has heard or lived through: sick baby, squabbling stepchildren, no clue what I could fix for dinner (that the kids would actually eat), and no energy to cook, anyway. No matter how many times I picked up the house, it still looked as if hungry raccoons had torn the place apart. The only solutions to my woes I could think of were to abandon the baby, strangle her brother and sister, torch the house, and leave my husband a note: "Have a good life. I'm outta here!"

Outside the window, the yard was covered with dandelions. My husband avoided yard work, and besides, he was too busy to do it. Since I was only working part-time and Paul's income as an assistant professor had to support two families, there wasn't money to hire anyone to weed and reseed the lawn. But those weeds bugged me. For days I had been glaring at the burgeoning dandelions as they grew bigger, bushier, and brighter, nearly overshadowing the grass. Telling myself that the yellow flowers made a beautiful carpet didn't seem to do the trick. I hated them.

On that day, as I looked out the window, I noticed that the whole crop had gone to seed. Hundreds of fluffy, white dandelion heads were spilling their seed all over the ground they didn't already cover. I couldn't stand the sight of them! They had become a symbol of my inability to bring order to my life. My whole life was out of control, a crazed dandelion patch gone to seed, about to spread millions of new weeds to cope with in the future. Somehow, I had to stop them!

Without a second thought, I put the baby in the kiddie backpack, told the older kids to go ahead and kill each other if they had to, grabbed the vacuum cleaner, and stormed out into the front yard. I pulled my husband's extra-long, heavy-duty power cord out of the carport and plugged the machine in. Charging back and forth across the lawn, I methodically vacuumed the entire front yard. Passersby stared. Neighbors peered out their doors, reluctant to ask any questions. But I didn't care. It felt so good to look at the denuded dandelions and to feel in charge of my life again.

And then I imagined what I must have looked like: an enraged lunatic marching back and forth across the yard with a squalling baby on her back, vacuuming up dandelion fluff. I began to laugh. And whenever I stopped laughing, this ludicrous image popped back into my mind and I started laughing all over again.

Except for the annihilated dandelions, nothing had changed. (It took us another five years to tear out most of the lawn and replace it with bushes.) But seeing the humor in what, moments before, had seemed like utter misery put an end to my temper tantrum and I could go on contentedly living my life the way it was.

—*Carolyn*

A VITAL LIFE FORCE

Humor is the "juice" of life. It affects us psychologically and physiologically. Having a sense of humor involves more than just telling jokes or being witty. It allows us to lift ourselves out of a rut by seeing things with fresh eyes and a good heart.

Laughter is nature's "high." It rejuvenates the body and the spirit. It relaxes your muscles, especially around your skeletal structure, erasing tension and knots. Laughter exercises the lungs and brings fresh air into your body. It stimulates circulation, essentially "cleaning house" for your system. The substances released in your body when you laugh are actually painkillers. When Norman Cousins treated his painful cancer with screenings of old Marx Brothers' movies, he found that laughter was exactly the right prescription. He describes this in his wonderful book, *Anatomy of an Illness* (Cousins, 1982).

MAGNETIZING MEETINGS

The ability to use humor effectively draws people to you. Knowing how to make others laugh creates a strong bond.

People like to be around you. It is as though you have a "park" around you that people can play in.

Often, men's meetings are, in my opinion, just too bloody serious. If you can pump humor into a dry meeting, you can reenergize the whole group, enhance creativity, and increase the likelihood that the members will come to the next meeting. Much can be gained by establishing norms for meetings that include allowing and encouraging people to relate amusing stories about themselves or tell jokes with a lighthearted, universal appeal (*not* put-downs!). It also helps if you can deliver bad news with wry humor.

One day Steffie's husband was teaching her how to fish. "We were fly casting on the Big Horn River in Wyoming," she recalls, "and as I attempted the tricky maneuver of 'double-hauling,' my line landed like a giant pile of spaghetti. I burst out laughing, while my husband scowled. Exasperated, I explained, 'If I can't laugh at myself, I'll throw in the towel and never learn!'"

Men and women tend to have different kinds of humor. As a rule, men prefer canned jokes, while women are amused by situational humor involving the ironies of life. Men use humor to stir things up, and women use it to smooth things out and put others at ease. Women often take the brunt of

Payoffs for Humor

▶ **You live longer.**

▶ **You have more friends.**

▶ **You inspire better results from others.**

▶ **You deal with difficult situations with added perspective and energy.**

▶ **You enjoy life more and are better equipped to lift the burdens from your own life and the lives of others.**

jokes to make others feel more comfortable, or to take someone else off the hook. Also, women are often more comfortable laughing at themselves. However, if you take on the role of the "fall guy" too often, you can discount yourself and lead others to do the same.

Another word of caution: Every one of us has been on the receiving end of malicious humor, when someone has used his or her intellect like a sword to wound us. Such humor does little but muddy the karmic pool. And those whom you make the objects of your derision, however funny you were at their expense, will very likely never forget, much less forgive you.

A Quick Wit Saves the Day

Jean Yancy, now in her seventies, is a business consultant with a long and successful career. She is also an entertaining and much sought-after public speaker. Once she was asked to speak to a group of eighteen hundred distinguished scientists. Following a glowing introduction by the emcee, Jean rose to walk to the podium, but she caught her heel on the carpet and sprawled across the speaker's platform, landing flat on her face. Using her automatic humor, this plump and motherly woman pulled herself to her feet and said, "Don't worry about a thing, folks. I just read my horoscope and it said I was going to take a long trip." The ability to laugh at ourselves is one of women's great gifts.

TOOLS OF EMPOWERMENT

Exercise   ### *SEVEN STEPS TO A LIGHTER HEART*

Practicing the following techniques will enhance your ability to use humor effectively and to learn to laugh at yourself and the world around you.

1. Be willing to risk the ridiculous. Laugh at yourself—after all, you above all others have the right to do so! When you laugh at yourself, it makes you very human and lovable, allowing those around you to relax and laugh with you.

2. Become aware of the things you do that tend to make you serious, angry, or depressed. Perhaps you listen to sad music, absorb yourself in real or fictitious dramas, or have critical, angry "talks" with yourself as you drive or work. If your mind is filled up with negative thoughts, it has no room for joyous, light, and humorous ones. When you catch yourself mired in negativity, make a conscious shift to seeing the humor in the very situation that was making you angry.

3. Deliberately look for the humor in every situation. Take time to observe life with your humor "glasses" on. Exaggerate that aspect in your mind. Even in a serious situation, you can step back and take a nonserious perspective for a moment. This is a skill you can practice anywhere—at meetings, waiting in line, stuck in traffic, in the throes of family activity. Very few things in life lack a funny side.

4. Saturate yourself with humor—with funny books, plays, and movies.

5. Foster laughter. Support humor when it happens. Encourage those around you when they say funny things that lighten everyone's day.

6. Look for what is beautiful and joyful in life. Acknowledging the good around you is not only a way of establishing a positive comparison in order to cheer yourself up; it lightens your heart as well.

7. Focus on developing a loving heart. True humor comes from love rather than anger.

Humor gives life its zest. It is like the gust of wind that sweeps a sailboat forward or the fresh idea that clears the cobwebs from your mind. Humorous women delight and engage those around them.

9

Harmony:

BRINGING YOUR MANY ROLES INTO HARMONY

❙❙*At work, you think of the children you have left at home. At home, you think of the work you've left unfinished. Such a struggle is unleashed within yourself. Your heart is rent.***❙❙**

—**Golda Meir**

❙❙*I seem to have an awful lot of people inside me.***❙❙**

—**Dame Edith Evans**

❙❙*I don't want to get to the end of my life and find that I just lived the length of it. I want to have lived the width of it as well.***❙❙**

—**Diane Ackerman**

S OMETIMES IT AMAZES ME how much living I can fit into one day. Yesterday was a good example. The day began conventionally enough, with twenty minutes of meditation and twenty minutes on my exercise bike. I had breakfast with a business associate to discuss a cable television project that would feature the work of two organizations I am involved with— a community hospital and my business.

At the office, I met with one of my partners to set some short-term priorities for her. Then I spent three hours with a creative consultant designing a training program. Following this session, he and I had a wonderful, spiritually renewing lunch, during which I got some help from him regarding my youngest son's current career dilemma. I took a moment to call my mother—who is in the hospital—to laugh and joke with her before visiting a new client to check on the progress of interviews for a custom training program we are creating for them.

Next I went to the airport to pick up my sister, who is also my business partner, and her daughter, who was returning home to convalesce from a serious auto accident in California. Not only did I want to show my love and support for my niece and my sister, but I wanted to assess my sister's state of mind and determine her ability to come back to work. My niece came off the plane with multiple fractures, including a broken leg and a crushed hand, and promptly announced that she had to go to the bathroom. Thus, the two women in the welcome party had to get her into the bathroom and onto a bedpan in her wheelchair, which turned out to be quite a challenging and hilarious enterprise.

From the airport I raced to meet my husband and accompanied him to our couples' therapy group (stopping for dinner at the fabulous McDonald's on the way!). We dealt with what makes an effective marriage from 7:00 to 10:00 P.M. From 10:00 to 11:00, I put on my hat as director of my husband's company and joined him in doing strategic planning with our business consultant.

Organizing my overflowing day required making choices and setting priorities. In terms of business activities,

I consciously decided to see the new client and work on the new training program, leaving the bulk of the ongoing business management issues for the following week's staff meeting. I chose to meet my sister and niece at the airport in lieu of visiting my mother in the hospital, since I had spent time with her there the night before.

Looking back on my day, I see that I covered all the critical bases. I could have exercised a little more—that's the one area I always skimp on. But I did devote some time to my physical well-being, as well as my spiritual life. I managed my roles as company president, community activist, mother, sister, and wife throughout the course of the day.

Not every day is like this—nor could it be! I spend most days in a more single-minded fashion. But we all have days like this one, and being able to cope with these times is a mark of empowerment. The challenge is to see that we fulfill our various roles without becoming scattered and worn-out.

—*Steffie*

HARMONY IS HARD-WON

Achieving this kind of harmony didn't come to me automatically. It was the result of a lot of struggling. A turning point came for me when I was thirty-six. My life at that point was in chaos. I felt obliged each day to do in twenty-four hours what should have taken me thirty-six. Each morning I got up and threw myself into the fray of my life's competing worlds: keeping my family and extended family happy (cooking, reading stories, chauffeuring, entertaining, and nurturing family members), caring for the household (cleaning, ironing, picking up after everyone, and doing yard work), and working. One thing was clear: I had no time for myself, and I was too busy to take the time to look at my life.

One day I found myself sitting at the end of the hallway, my knees under my chin, weeping. I was exhausted, angry, feeling sorry for myself, and totally out of control. For some unexplained reason, but probably spurred by survival instinct, I took that afternoon and evening to evaluate what

I was doing. The first decision I made was to be more selfish (that is how I looked at it) and the next was to be more demanding of others. I was twisting myself into a pretzel to meet everyone else's needs and not asking for the things *I* needed.

My life was chock-full of family, work and running the house. I knew I couldn't add anything else to it until I disciplined myself to take the time (not make the time) to do so. My first move was to declare "bathroom time" for mom. This was my sacred time to fill the bathtub and read for at least half an hour. No one was allowed to knock on the door, yell through the door, or intrude on me in any way. (This included telling my youngest child to stop poking his fingers under the door to let me know he was waiting for me to hurry up and finish my bath.)

The next thing I did was to look at yard work in a different way. No more cutting the grass, hauling dirt, and so on. If my husband wasn't going to do it, we would just have to live in a jungle. *My* job, which I redefined as a privilege, was to plant and tend the flower and vegetable gardens. (You can do that and still hear the birds and marvel at nature.) When I got home from work, I renewed myself by spending time in my garden. This change in perspective had a "Tom Sawyer" effect on my husband and we spent some wonderful weekends canning vegetables and creating flower arrangements together.

Being an inveterate adventurer, I would declare "independent holidays" when the kids and I would select an adventure—playing in the creek, going to movies and the museum, or taking a trip to the amusement park. It was much more fun if we did this during school time, to give it a sense of secret drama. Our weekly budget of five dollars for these outings stimulated our creativity.

Then I began a regular practice of looking at my life, developing a pattern that included brief "time outs"— moments when I would call a friend, drive through the park, or sit in my office and watch the sun set for half an hour. This practice has evolved over the years into a discipline of ensuring that each day includes not only moments of renewal, but learning times, fun times, and focused times.

Another lesson I learned about a harmonious life was that I shouldn't think it would be free of stress, difficulty, or tears. So when events arise that bring the less welcome "notes" in the song of my life, I embrace them rather than resisting. I cry when I am moved. I let people know when I am angry with them and why. When I am stressed out, I take walks, get enough sleep, watch what I eat, drop more items to the "later" list, and concentrate on taking good care of myself.

Harmony comes from disciplining your life the way an athlete does. Just getting up in the morning and marching off to get everything done doesn't suffice. Such a life has no choices, only burdens. Harmonious living looks different at different times in your life. At my age, I am able to have a day like the one I described at the start of this chapter. But it would never have been possible to do that if I hadn't established control as a regular practice throughout my life.

THREE MYTHS ABOUT HARMONY

Myth No. 1: Harmony Means Balance

Balance implies that the roles you are juggling have equal status or weight, which is false. Think of life as a set of notes, combined into a beautiful, complex song. Your work life, spiritual life, and family life are all notes to be played. As you learn new notes throughout your life, the tune will change, but it is important to ensure that all your notes are played. You need to put into your song the notes that you value. A key note is solitude. Sometimes, when you are learning a new movement in the musical composition that is your life, you'll hit a few "clinkers"; this is a normal period of adjustment as you move forward and grow. You need to acquire an ear for the tune of your life. Is it discordant? Is the tune static? Are you sick of hearing it? Your song must evolve as you move through your life.

Myth No. 2: Harmony Means "Having It All"

We tend to think of success in terms of having it all, all at once. This is impossible, a bill of goods that many American women have been sold—or have sold themselves. It is as ridiculous as attempting to play all the keys on a piano simultaneously. At different stages of your life, different notes will necessarily be more important. Your career may carry the tune in your younger years, while you may shift to a family theme at a later time, or vice versa. This is perfectly okay.

Myth No. 3: Harmony Means Being Able to Please Others

In fact, harmony means making hard choices and sometimes cutting others out of your life for a time. What is important is being the composer of your *own* life, rather than merely singing someone else's tune, so you can sing your song with pride and with your whole heart. Anne Morrow Lindbergh wrote: "Traditionally we are taught, and instinctively we long, to give where it is needed—and immediately. Eternally, woman spills herself away in driblets to the thirsty, seldom being allowed the time, the quiet, the peace, to let the pitcher fill up to the brim" (Lindbergh, 1975, p. 45).

SOLOS AND RESTS

A potential pitfall for women comes from the fact that for them, the nurturing note predominates. It is more socially acceptable for men to be self-absorbed. Women can go wrong by not being focused enough on themselves. A friend was shocked to realize that she spent virtually no time alone. She used her daily planner to create harmony in her life by actually booking time for herself. One evening a week was hers alone, and she made a rule that she would allow nothing and no one to encroach upon her time during those evenings. Sometimes these kinds of drastic measures are required to bring harmony back into your life.

When Carolyn had a full-time private practice as a psychotherapist, she worked four ten-hour days and took Wednesday off. "I spent that day alone doing personal and household chores," she says. "For me, it was relaxing to be alone all day, and to know that more of my weekend could be spent with my family and friends instead of doing chores."

HARMONY WITH OTHERS

It is just as important not to sing so loudly that you drown out others' songs. Sometimes, you have to pay close attention to be able to tune in to their shifting priorities. In this way, you can influence them or blend your melody with theirs. Steffie says, "When a long time passes and I hear nothing from my youngest son, that's a red flag. When I hear a lot from my oldest son, that's a cause for concern, since he is normally very self-reliant. When my husband keeps singing the same tune over and over, I know I have to confront him about it or our relationship will get out of whack. Consciously observing these signs so I can focus my attention where it's needed helps me preserve harmony with the important people in my life."

KNOW YOUR LIMITS

It's important to remember that some people simply have more energy than others. You just have to know yourself, and know your own limits. "For years, I struggled with feelings of inferiority and anger because I simply couldn't do as much as my sister did," Carolyn laments. "I can get tired and depressed just listening to women like her review their schedules! I have always worked too hard, trying to cram as much in a day as I can. Certainly, I have many interests and passions I want to pursue. To do half of what my sister does and end up exhausted is so frustrating! Our family joke is that the Creator accidentally gave me her share of 'bosom,' but gave her my portion of physical energy. Perhaps I was destined to languish half-dressed on a chaise like a Rubens

Venus, while Steffie dashes about the forest in perpetual motion as Diana, goddess of the hunt. I've never accepted that fate with much grace or good cheer, but the truth is that I burn out much more quickly, I get sick more easily, and after a certain point, I am no longer effective.

"I have to keep reminding myself that even high-energy women have to make hard choices, keep their lives in harmony, and take care of themselves. When I begin to compare myself unfavorably to other women in terms of accomplishments, I switch my attention to the very real sense of satisfaction I have with my life just as it is at that moment. Gradually, I have come to feel grateful about this aspect of my nature, because it has forced me to develop a more inwardly focused life. Meditation and contemplation don't sap my energy the way more externally focused activities do. Quite the opposite. They renew and revitalize me."

KNOW YOUR SONG

Remember to focus on the big picture, the entire musical score, rather than getting lost in individual notes that may be difficult for you to play. Reflect on what you are trying to get done. What is your overriding purpose and vision for your life? How do the activities that fill up your day, your week, and your month support that purpose and vision? Beware of fanciful trills and flourishes among your life notes that play no part in furthering your life's direction. Your time is precious.

That said, it is still important to factor in fun as part of your daily schedule. At the end of her long day, Steffie and her husband, giggling and wielding flashlights, pirated dead flowers from a park for a dried-flower bouquet. As you start each day, ask yourself what will be hard and what will be fun. Save your energy for the hard things, but remember to revel in the fun.

The Life of a Virtuoso

Linda Nelson is a vice president at Gensler & Associates Architects, the largest design firm in the country, and

Payoffs for Harmony

▶ You have peace of mind.

▶ You increase your ability to grow and handle more complicated tunes.

▶ You are less affected by stress.

▶ You feel that life is more worthwhile.

▶ You gain an ever-renewed sense of personal accomplishment.

▶ You successfully combine creativity and practicality.

managing principal of the firm's Denver office. The design field is fast-paced and competitive; those who succeed must be well attuned to clients' needs and anticipate obstacles to good service. Linda's work days are filled with travel, management, marketing, and goodwill building.

Despite this rigorous schedule, she maintains an air of quietude and openness that is reassuring to her clients and colleagues. She devotedly takes off one month every year to pursue her avocation—deep-sea diving, a skill she has perfected enough to have been included on a diving expedition with Jean-Michel Cousteau. Her other passion is exploring developing countries in order to get a sense of how others live. These travels have given her a unique perspective that has led to empathetic insights into human behavior, which in turn have assisted her in managing people at Gensler.

Although Linda has no immediate family, her ties with her primary relatives are nurturing and continuous. She writes her parents once a week, spends ski vacations with her nephews, and makes the trip home for every major holiday. Linda's nurturing qualities extend to her employees, who feel guided by her fair yet steady hand, which supports them as they grow.

In her search for harmony between work and a spiritual life, Linda recently purchased land in western Colorado and built a small cabin for herself. In this setting, away from the urban environment, she spends time pursuing the gifts of solitude. The combination of her rich inner life and her business skills enhances her effectiveness on the job.

TOOLS OF EMPOWERMENT

Exercise — *LOGGING YOUR LIFE*

There is no better way to discover the presence or absence of harmony in your life than to become clear about how you really spend your time. Create a simple chart, with columns for "Activity," "Time of Day," "Total Time," and "Role." A partial example is shown here.

Activity	Time of Day	Total Time	Role
Up, read paper	5:30–6:00	30 mins.	Personal
Walk dog	6:00–6:30	30 mins.	Family member
Shower, dress	6:30–7:15	45 mins.	Personal
Straighten house	7:15–7:45	30 mins.	House manager
Breakfast, travel	7:45–9:00	1 hr., 15 mins.	Personal
Work	9:00–5:00	8 hrs.	Employee

After completing a time log for several days, you can analyze it in several ways. Examine which roles dominate in terms of the time spent. Then compare your daily activities with your values list. (See Chapter Fourteen.) Do your activities reflect your goals?

Total the hours spent in various categories, then draw a pie chart reflecting these totals as percentages. This visual portrayal of how you spend your time can be very enlightening, and you may find that you want to make a change. A woman in our workshop, for example, was astonished to realize that she spent thirty-eight hours a week watching television.

Exercise   *CLEANING HOUSE*

Make a commitment to clean out the sour notes in your life, activities that don't reward you and people who damage you.

Here is an example: We all have relationships with people who are "takers." At some point we may have to quietly drop them from our lives or take a stand with them. For example, you might have to say, "Look. For the past four years, we've been talking about your rotten marriage and nothing has happened. It seems as if I haven't been helpful and I'm tired of hearing about it endlessly. I don't want to talk about it anymore." This gives you the possibility of preserving the relationship without having to endure the one aspect you find unpleasant.

Employers often comment to us that a great strength of female employees is that they are flexible; they know how to juggle many roles and tasks. While this is a great asset for ourselves, our bosses, and our families, we can also take this tendency too far, once more trying to do it all. As an antidote, here's a six-step exercise for cleaning out and prioritizing your activities:

1. List all the activities you are involved in right now, both daily and occasionally. Include all areas of your life: jobs, running a household, doing errands, volunteer activities, sports, entertainment, church activities, personal care, and so on. Be specific, and put down everything you can think of.

2. Put an "M" beside each activity that represents a true obligation—a "must do." Put a "J" beside each activity that brings you joy. Some items may not fit in either category; others may go into both.

3. Circle each item that did not fall into either category. For each item, think about why you are doing it. Do you have a false sense of responsibility? Is it just a leftover habit?

Are you afraid you'll hurt somebody's feelings? Write your answer next to the item. Ask yourself if it could be dropped altogether, or handed off to a co-worker, family member, or friend.

4. Review your "must do" list. Go through the same process as above. Then examine whether you could delegate or renegotiate any of these activities with family members or co-workers, or hire someone to do them.

5. Think about what you need to do to reduce the number of activities in your life. Write down the action steps required and write the first step in your appointment book.

6. Commit to making these changes in your life.

Exercise   *APATHY / SYMPATHY / EMPATHY*

We can get out of harmony by overly involving ourselves in other people's lives, squandering our energy by giving immediately and fully to others. This not only drains us dry; it also disempowers others by making them dependent on us. We have to prioritize our commitments. As Anne Morrow Lindbergh warns, "With our pitchers, we attempt sometimes to water a field, not a garden" (Lindbergh, 1975, p. 52).

The first step in preserving our energy is to pick our battles wisely. When we are clear about our vision, values, and goals, it is much easier to discern when we must turn away from something. We must also know our limits in terms of time, energy, interest, caring, money, and other resources. And we have to know who we are and are not to know what we can and can't do. Armed with this self-awareness, we can find that balance point where we are neither too involved with others nor too self-absorbed.

Apathy: The Disinterested Bystander

There are certain issues or people we just can't expend our energy on, today or perhaps indefinitely. When we can't engage in a situation, we respond apathetically. *Apathy* is simply turning away from a person or a situation out of a lack of interest or feeling for it. The disinterested bystander has checked her values and her priorities, and she:

- Simply doesn't care

- Is disinterested, not engaged with this person or issue

- Doesn't need to be involved here

Her motto is: "It's not my battle."

Once we pick our battles, we need to know how to engage properly so that we can hope for some positive outcome: a true win-win situation for ourselves and others. Here it is important to know the difference between *sympathy* and *empathy*.

Sympathy: The Misguided Heroine

Watch out for sympathy. It is a bottomless pit of quicksand that pulls you and the other person down! The misguided heroine gets completely caught up in another's problems; she:

- Feels the same pain

- Puts no limits on her helpfulness

- Takes on the other person's problems to solve herself

- Sees and reinforces the other person as a victim who is disempowered

Her motto is: "There must be a way to fix it and it's up to me to find it."

Empathy: The Caring Consultant

In contrast to sympathy, empathy is a heartfelt, yet measured and truly helpful response to a person in pain. The caring consultant feels for others, but doesn't lose herself by taking on their pain or barging in to "fix" their lives. She maintains her own boundaries so that she simply assists the other person as she:

- Appreciates the other person's pain

- Sets limits on her helpfulness (the resources she will expend)

- Leaves the responsibility for solving the problem with the other person

- Sees and treats the other person as capable of running his or her own life and as empowered

Her motto is: "Win, lose, or draw, it's *your* life."

Moving Toward Empathy

Many clues are available for determining which role you are playing in a particular situation with a particular person. Several are listed below.

Clues for Sympathy

In helping someone out of *sympathy,* you find yourself:

- Agreeing with the other person's negative views
- Giving a lot of advice
- Making statements such as "You should do . . ."
- Feeling that you are powerful and competent and the other person is helpless ("Poor thing . . .")
- Treating the other person as if he or she is incompetent
- Taking over
- Taking on the other person's pain
- Feeling frustrated and anxious
- Doing all the work
- Spinning your wheels
- At the end of the conversation, feeling either smug or exhausted, angry or depressed

In *sympathy,* you find the person you are helping:

- Becoming helpless
- Acting dumb
- Resisting your advice or suggestions
- Whining
- Only going through the motions of following your advice

- Getting more upset

- Passively agreeing with you

- Asking you a lot of questions

- Still feeling bad at the end of the conversation

Clues for Empathy

In *empathy*, you find yourself guiding another person toward possible solutions by:

- Treating him or her as competent

- Asking a lot of questions

- Giving only occasional advice

- Sharing your own experiences instead

- Maintaining your own emotional state in the face of the other person's pain

- Feeling strong, calm, and "centered"

- Helping the other person discover personal resources for self-help

- Pointing the other person toward other resources—books, experts, information

- Affirming the person's positive qualities

- Asking the other person when and how he or she has solved a similar problem

- Offering only what you can give with goodwill

- At the end of the conversation, feeling energized, as if your time and energy have been well spent

In *empathy*, you find the other person:

- Acting competent

- Lightening up and calming down

- Realizing that there are already some solutions at hand

- Feeling affirmed

- Telling you what he or she knows

- Joking about his or her predicament

- Coming up with at least a few steps toward a solution

- Making plans and decisions

- Feeling better at the end of the conversation

Note: Sometimes people aren't ready to move on yet, and in those instances nothing you do will make a difference to them, but at least if you are being empathetic, you won't be unhappy too!

To work on moving from helping someone out of sympathy and into helping out of empathy, follow these steps:

1. Identify a situation where you feel you have gotten overly involved with someone else's problem. Even if you are consistently empathetic in most areas of your life, you are bound to find at least one situation where you are, or have been, mired down in sympathy. You are most likely to get hooked into the problem of someone you love or feel sorry for, someone who makes you feel guilty.

2. Review the *Clues for Sympathy* and note which ones apply to you in that situation.

3. Write down specific examples of when and how you fell into each behavior.

4. Review the *Clues for Empathy* and think about how you could move from being the Misguided Heroine to being the Caring Consultant with this person. Design an action plan to change your approach, and set a specific time to take the first step.

If you are aware of the events and people that trigger disharmony in your life, you can stay on track. Striving to live your life according to your highest priorities gives you a growing sense of empowerment and self-esteem.

10

Receptivity:

HAVING AN OPEN MIND

❞*Tolerance implies no lack of commitment to one's own beliefs. Rather it condemns the oppression or persecution of others.***❞**
                                          —**John F. Kennedy**

❞*When two people in a business always agree, one of them is unnecessary.***❞**
                                          —**Anonymous**

❞*All change in the quality of people's lives must grow out of a change in their visions of reality.***❞**
                                          —**John Powell**

MY HUSBAND'S PARENTS SWEAR THAT his first words were "How it works?" They were reportedly spoken as he toddled around the house pointing at every mechanical device in sight—early evidence that he viewed the world from the perspective of an engineer. In contrast, I seem to have always had the same curiosity about people. My mother says that I constantly asked questions about everyone we met ("Why does he frown so much?" "Is her grandma nice to her?" "Do they have children?"). While my mother sees this fascination with people as a blessing, my daughter has always regarded it as a source of embarrassment, particularly when she was a teenager. "Mom, you're staring at that woman!" she would hiss at me as we stood in line at the movies. "Why do you ask my friends so many questions?" she would rage after her friends left the house. I could only protest, "What do you expect from a psychologist? I'm interested in people!"

Seeing life from many perspectives has been critical to my work, and being a psychologist has continually developed my ability to see the world through other people's eyes. Every session with a client extends my understanding and, more importantly, allows me to put that knowledge to work as a coach, guide, and resource person. When I work with a teenager and her parents, for example, seeing the conflict from all of their individual perspectives allows me to "translate" them to each other. Knowing that someone else's view makes sense, even if you don't agree with it, is a critical step toward resolving conflicts. Of course, the value of this knowledge carries over into my interactions with my own daughter and helps me to understand when she is upset with me.

In spite of this, certain perspectives are much harder for me to assume than others. The more different people's lives are from mine, the more disparate their values, the more I have to stretch to find the common experience that will open a door into their world. My husband's engineering perspective was one of the hardest ones for me to adopt. The minute something went wrong, I would cry, "I don't like machines!" Eventually, I realized how much it was costing me and others for me to refuse to understand machines, particularly my much-used computer. So I began to think about my little laptop computer and tiny portable printer as cute domestic animals who devotedly did their duty day in and day out. I began to handle them gently, even talk to them sweetly, as I would treat a faithful pet. Weird . . . maybe. But I have to say, the machines work better now and I don't get as upset when something breaks down.

We all have some perspectives that click in more naturally than others. They spring from our interests, our values, our upbringing, and the experiences we've had in our many different roles in life. However, by becoming aware of our perspectives and being willing to expand or reorder them, we can work much more effectively with others. Doing this also keeps us open to changing our own outlooks.

—Carolyn

REWEAVING THE TAPESTRY

Since our perspective is the means by which we make sense of the world, day by day and hour by hour, it is naturally challenged at times. There are moments in life when our perspective is blasted apart by an experience or a bit of new knowledge, forcing us to reconstruct the framework—to repair the tapestry, if you will—in order to make sense of things again. We are all driven to be in harmony with our perspective.

The causes for such a revision, or reordering, of the threads can be varied. Growing up or learning something new are the most common perspective-shifting phenomena that happen to us. Major life experiences, especially crises, can suddenly and totally turn our view of the world upside down. The premature death of a parent can throw a family into tumult, for example. Divorce can impact one's lifestyle, attitude about money, goals, and entire sense of what is meaningful. Even a great achievement can alter our perspective on ourselves and the world around us.

History is filled with examples of one-time "truths" that were later debunked. If you keep yourself open to questioning your assumptions, and to fine-tuning and enhancing your understanding, you remain in step with the fast-changing world. Your perspective inevitably changes as you attempt to make meaning out of your life. And the greater your capacity for seeing the same event from other perspectives, the greater your power to deal with it.

In our increasingly diverse society, viewing life from many perspectives is not just an advantage, it is a *must*. If we are going to make the most of the diversity in our own communities, let alone enter into business deals with members of the European marketplace or merchants from the Pacific Rim, we must have the ability to step into many other people's shoes, and to see the world as they see it.

JUDGE—BUT JUDGE WELL!

The first—and perhaps the most difficult—requirement for accommodating others' perspectives is the ability and willingness to suspend judgment at the outset. This is a big challenge, because you have created your own perspective over the course of your entire life. That perspective is the framework that holds your beliefs—beliefs about what is right and wrong, what is important and what isn't, and what pleases or angers you. As you try to understand someone else's perspective, your own will be challenged, which may make you angry, confused, and impatient—or maybe just surprised. At that moment it is difficult, yet important, to suspend your automatic judgmental response. It is vital to remember that your rules for operating are perspectives, habits, and customs—not fundamental truths.

STOP MAKING SENSE

Logic may or may not be useful to this exercise in understanding. For example, after learning about someone's religion we may understand why he or she eats certain foods or celebrates certain holidays. But logic will not explain why some people believe in reincarnation and others believe in an eternal life in heaven or hell. Nor will the logic of one believer make much of an impact on those who hold another belief. What is important is to recognize and value our differences and similarities. How much of another person's perspective you adopt is strictly your decision. For example, if you are a Western woman, you may find it difficult to accept the life-style of Muslim women. You may feel angry and disap-pointed that they do not respond to the "freedoms" you think they should desire. But respect is the issue here, not logic.

CULTIVATING COMPASSION

We may need to deal with roles and circumstances that we can never make our own. We cannot change our race or gender. Having had an education, we cannot experience what it would be like not to have had one. In these areas, we need an empathetic and intellectual understanding to "translate" other people's experiences into our own perspective.

Also, just because we have not experienced something does not invalidate other people's differing experiences. For example, one of our client companies is billed as a "woman-friendly" organization. A high-level female employee of this company talks enthusiastically about how the company promotes, trains, and listens to its female employees. But a woman working in another area of the same company speaks with anger and discouragement about how the five women in her area are forced to accept the way men see and do things. "To practice law here," she says, "you have to be a 'junkyard dog,' tough, mean, and aggressive." Although this woman saw many opportunities for saving the company time and money by creating a work environment based on the devel-opment of relationships, no one other than her female peers would even listen to her.

Each woman thought the other one was wrong in her appraisal of the firm; however, in terms of their own expe-riences of the company and their views of what "woman-friendly" meant, both descriptions were accurate. It's not a matter of deciding which one of them was "correct." A neutral observer, listening to both women, might describe the company as having pockets of woman-friendliness.

KNOW YOUR BLIND SPOTS

Beware of your biases. If your awareness is dulled or uneducated, you may entirely miss what your experience means to others. One of our seminar participants stated that women were not discriminated against in her company, and that anyone who wanted to work hard could get ahead there. Several things were obvious to everyone who listened to her. First, her definition of working hard was putting in a sixty-hour week, which she accepted as normal. Furthermore, she was married to a man who worked as many hours as she did, and they had no children. Finally, she was in an industry in which many women worked, but most were at the bottom of the ladder. A few, like herself, had moved to the top due to a forward-thinking and pioneering president. While she was an exception to the rule, the rule remained as a barrier for others.

Her message was "Be like me and you can get ahead." She was blind to the experience of others. What of the woman with three children who couldn't or wouldn't sacrifice them to a sixty-hour work week? Or the women who didn't have husbands whose incomes allowed them to pursue the training they needed, take job risks, and hire help at home? This woman took for granted many of the factors in her own success. She believed that she had made it on her own, and that "anyone could." Other women's experiences were simply beyond her understanding.

Fully knowing your own perspective and learning about those of other people is the genius of the diplomat. This does not require you to give up your own perspective or agree with someone else's. In fact, our own perspective is the firmest ground on which we stand. Understanding another person's perspective allows us to challenge or disagree with it, knowing *why* we do.

Payoffs for Receptivity

▶ **You have a better idea of how to get your own ideas across.**

▶ **You enrich your own views and add to your ability to solve problems and to enjoy the world around you.**

▶ **Understanding reduces fear, bigotry, and prejudice.**

▶ **You work more effectively with others because you understand their issues and concerns more clearly.**

▶ **You see the limitations of your own way of doing things, thereby expanding your knowledge of who you are and who you are not.**

Wearing Many Frames of Reference

Gail Schoettler, treasurer of the State of Colorado, provides a fine working example of how viewing life from many perspectives can make you a more powerful and effective person. Gail served on the school board in Douglas County. She told us that her ability to look at school board issues through the eyes of a mother, a businesswoman, a government official, and an economist—all roles she had played—assisted her in understanding the specific interest groups that interacted with the board. While she didn't always agree with them, these groups knew that she understood their frames of reference because she had spent some time personally exploring each one and could express their points of view.

From Gail's story, you can see how politics is a vivid example of an arena in which you need to understand and accurately represent many viewpoints. This is necessary in order to clarify people's positions and find common ground, enabling a group to come to a consensus or at least allowing you to know who will be unhappy with a given decision and why. Understanding different perspectives is just as important in running a meeting, resolving a dispute between upset children, making a sale, or living comfortably with a roommate.

TOOLS OF EMPOWERMENT

Exercise   LEARNING FROM OTHERS

To appreciate women with different perspectives from yours, read books or rent videotapes about women whose personality, values, race, or culture differ from your own. As you become acquainted with a particular woman, notice what really is different and what you have in common. Imagine having a conversation with this woman on a subject that you consider to be of great concern to all women. To test whether you really understand both viewpoints, speak both voices or even write out the dialogue you would have with the other person.

Exercise   LOOKING IN ON YOURSELF

To become aware of your own perspectives and to practice bringing them to bear on a problem by choice, make a list of all the roles you play in your life: sister, banker, den mother, world citizen, board member, and so on. Take a specific problem and think it through by looking at it from each perspective, moving from one role to the next. Get a job or volunteer for a project that will put you in an entirely different milieu and that you will have to learn quickly in order to make a contribution.

Exercise *GETTING UNSTUCK*

Your personal perspective has two aspects: your worldview (how you believe the world to be) and your inner view (how you believe yourself to be). Your inner perspective can either help or hinder your efforts to learn about yourself. Particularly when you are fearful or depressed, you are most likely to be closed in, stuck, and unwilling to take a fresh look at things. Yet it is that very shift in perspective that will help you get going again. The following are some ways to assess your own openness:

- Can you *listen*, setting your judgments aside for a while to take in the information, feelings, and motivations of others?

- Can you *observe*, again temporarily setting your judgments aside? A good exercise for developing this skill is to ride a bus and observe your fellow passengers. Be aware of the things you see that trigger your defenses or judgments. Note them and put them aside. Keep working on this until you can become an open observer.

- Do you hear yourself frequently saying, "Yes, but . . ." (meaning "You're right, but I'm *more* right")? Do you have to have an answer or opinion on everything? These are signals that you are cutting others off, or even out, of your world. You may be inadvertently losing the opportunity to gain other people's perspective and wisdom. Instead, when you find yourself cutting others off, stop, ask questions, and listen to the answers. When you are clear where the other person stands and where you stand, you can either say "I don't know" or take a strong position without feeling defensive.

Once again, asking people you trust to give you honest feedback about how they think you see the world can be an excellent learning device. You could ask, "What are some of my assumptions about life? People? Work? Relationships? Morality? Religion? Fun?" You probably know people who always see things in a positive light and others who are good at seeing what could go wrong. In the same way, you present your perspective to others through what you say and do, and they may help you to see it better than you can alone.

A trainer of top athletes routinely interviews candidates for his services to determine which ones he will work with. Although it appears to the athletes that he is merely "shooting the breeze" with them, he is actually listening for their perspective. Through their words and body language, some of the candidates are sending the messages "I work hard," "I can do it," or "I'll do what it takes to be the best."

What do *your* words and behavior say? They are the keys to your perspective.

Exercise   *EXPLORING YOUR WORLDVIEW*

The more you know about your own perspective, the easier it is to remain open to those of other people because you have a standard against which to compare them. Much of who we are comes from our culture, which influences our attitudes, beliefs, values, and experiences. It provides a context in which we adopt roles, religious concepts, forms of speech, customs, knowledge, jobs, governmental and organizational structures, songs and art forms, recreation, food, and dress. It spells out our choices, right down to our hairstyles, socially appropriate ways of looking at others, and even prescribed tone of voice.

Discover *your* current worldview. A simple way to begin is by filling in the blanks in the following sentences:

- I see the world as being _____.
- I believe people are _____.
- Spirituality is _____.
- The material things in life are _____.
- To me, life is _____.
- I believe I am _____.

Add any other categories that work for you. (You may want to include areas such as environment, family, or justice.) Include your vision once you have completed that section of this book; it is a core part of your perspective.

Put your list aside for a few days after you're through writing. Then come back to it to look for themes and key words that will allow you to write a summary statement of your worldview. Such a statement might look like this:

I see the world as being unjust. To me, the world is a place to learn and grow. Growth may be joyous, painful, easy, hard, scary, or exciting. The point is to learn the lessons it offers while respecting the inherent goodness in people.

I see life as an adventure, some of which has prescribed paths, and other parts of which are new and unexplored. It's important to have stimulating companions along the way. One should always question the path.

Once you have an awareness of how you see life, you can work to suspend that perspective to explore someone else's. Contrasting your perspective with other people's allows you to explore the limitations it may hold for you.

Exercise *DETECTIVE WORK*

To better understand the perspective of someone different from you, try the following total-immersion method. First, decide that you want to learn the other person's perspective. Then, immerse yourself completely in the "culture" of that point of view long enough to understand it—as an observer, not a critic. For example, to learn the business perspective, spend time with businesspeople to see what they talk about, what their concerns are, and what motivates them.

You can use this technique on a smaller scale, too. At a party, a committee meeting, or even the family dinner table, imagine yourself in the place of someone whose viewpoint is different from your own. Think about how you would feel, what opinions you would express, and how you would interact with the others present. You will learn a lot in a very short time.

Constantly practicing an open-minded outlook enhances your ability to solve problems, make decisions, and communicate effectively with others. It keeps your intellect limber and your life receptive to change.

Accountability:

TAKING RESPONSIBILITY
FOR YOUR LIFE

❚❚ *Full maturity . . . is achieved by realizing that you have choices to make.* **❚❚**

         —Angela Barron McBride

❚❚ *Take your life in your own hands and what happens? A terrible thing: no one to blame.* **❚❚**

         —Erica Jong

❚❚ *I'm not going to limit myself just because people won't accept the fact that I can do something else.* **❚❚**

         —Dolly Parton

127

F OR MANY YEARS, I WAS MARRIED to a very successful man. From all appearances, he was an ideal husband and excellent provider for his family, who treated us to the country club life. However, he was also a controlling, domineering person, which began to affect how our two small sons and I interacted with him. I developed ruses for surviving in what had become an unbearable situation. For example, after a day out, I would rush to beat him home. I would set up the ironing board, turn on the iron, and position a pile of clothes nearby. Then I would cook up something aromatic, like onions. All so that my domesticity would seem to be beyond reproach.

One day as I stepped out of the shower, I felt terribly dizzy. As I lunged for the towel rack to steady myself, the admonition "To thine own self be true" came into my head. It seemed very significant, but I wasn't sure how. Over the next three months I contemplated the meaning of those words and I slowly realized that I had to divorce my husband. My attempts to make our marriage work over the years had failed. The choice before me was to be true to myself and take control of my life or to surrender to his will. The latter alternative felt like a flagrant breach of my own integrity.

I began setting goals. Since everything was in my husband's name, I took steps to establish my own credit. I talked with lawyers about my options. I sat down and listed all the negative implications of the divorce—the friends I would lose, the clubs I wouldn't belong to, the life-style changes I would experience—as well as the pluses. Because I was certain that I wanted sole custody of the children, I made arrangements for them to talk with a child psychologist. I sought support from my family. And I systematically searched for a job so I wouldn't need alimony, only child support. All of these steps were designed to erase my dependency on my husband.

The first part of my break for freedom was acknowledging that my marital situation was out of alignment with who I was. My life goals didn't match my husband's. I also wanted to raise my children in a healthy environment—even though it might be unconventional. I knew I had to take action to reestablish harmony within myself. I needed to find a job that supported me and that allowed me to contribute to the community. I needed to help my kids understand what I was doing. (One of them had no problems, and the other was helped for a while by the psychologist). As I began to put all these things in motion, I became accountable for my future.

The premise of accountability is that power rests within you, not outside of you. You are not a victim. Yes, terrible things can and do happen, but when they do, the empowered woman feels she has a choice about how to respond.

I know a woman who has allowed her entire life to be defined by the rape she experienced nearly thirty years ago. Another rape victim almost immediately handled it by viewing it as an *attempted* degradation, something that happened to her body but that could not touch her soul. In each case, a horrible event occurred, but these two women responded very differently to it. The essential thing is recognizing that you control the impact events have in your life, rather than feeling as though you are controlled by them.

—Steffie

BLUEPRINTS FOR YOUR DREAMS

As we discussed in Chapter Six, your vision provides a framework for your life. Once you have formulated your vision, you can do three things to take responsibility for the form and direction your life takes:

1. Set goals.

2. Set limits.

3. Make conscious decisions.

People who get what they want don't do it unconsciously. If you don't set your own goals, you are in danger of being pulled into accomplishing someone else's—or having none at all. But oh, the resistance to setting goals! It's so formal, so restrictive. The mind conjures up dozens of excuses. The truth is that in writing down what you really want, you are making a commitment to yourself. No more fudging. You either take on your own life or admit that you don't have the courage. Setting goals is a way of measuring your progress. Goals are necessary to put your feet in motion, and to prevent yourself from living forever in the realm of pipe dreams.

CROSSOVER GOALS

Corporate women who come into our training have often experienced what we call "goals till you gag," because there is such an emphasis on goal training in business. Nevertheless, they have seldom considered having goals in areas such as adding fun into their life, spending more time with their families, or pursuing some kind of personal passion. In addition, they sometimes haven't known how to connect work goals with their own self-interest. When one very career-oriented woman realized this, she developed a work goal of learning to effectively delegate so that she would never have to stay at the office beyond 5:00 P.M. The payoff was that she could spend some fun time with her kids instead of merely nagging them for a few minutes each night to get their homework and chores done. The woman, her supervisor, and her family all benefited from this "work" goal because she had a personal reason for setting it.

Many women new to the professional world, or those who have focused on volunteer work or homemaking, have either given little thought to goals or have never considered what they want to accomplish in their lives, much less how to do it. We have seen life open up in exciting new directions for women who consider this for the first time.

PARING DOWN THE POSSIBILITIES

After formalizing your goals, you will need to set limits, both for yourself and for others, in order to remain focused. If your goal has to do with your career, this can take the form of refusing to do others' tasks at work or only taking on jobs you are qualified for or are competent to complete. It may mean skipping your child's soccer game, saying no to a friend's request, turning down a volunteer assignment, or forgoing homemade supper.

Setting limits means setting boundaries that are inviolable by you or others. Examples include conserving your physical energy, getting out of relationships that are physically or emotionally abusive, and setting parameters for how you will and will not be treated. This last one is difficult. Often your family expects you to behave in certain ways, such as being conciliatory or outspoken. You have to be honest about yourself and know if you are unwittingly inviting certain kinds of abuse. Setting limits takes self-knowledge and discipline.

Again, an important element of setting limits involves communicating clearly with others, stating your expectations, monitoring them, and renegotiating if they are not met. It is important to be honest about your boundaries up front. This may mean telling your employer that you can't work late because you have a small child at home. You have a legitimate right to balk when you feel your time, money, work efficiency, or family life are being threatened or invaded. This is sometimes difficult for women because it seems to violate their tradition of caretaking. But caring for others is not always the highest priority; sometimes self-preservation comes first.

MAKING DECISIONS

Being decisive is a big challenge for women. We have long gotten a subtle message that says, "Yes, you're competent, but you can't handle responsibility as well as a man. You can't make tough decisions."

It is frightening how haphazardly some women make vital decisions in their lives. Josie told us that when she married, her gut told her up until the wedding day that it wouldn't work, but she ignored the message. Five years later, she was divorced, but not surprised. Roxanne shared the information that she had never belabored big decisions in her life, but always acted impulsively. In retrospect, she felt that she had paid dearly for this pattern. Betty, who said that she always relied on her intuition and never bothered to assess the facts of a situation, regrets important decisions she made that way.

STARRY-EYED AND WRONG-HEADED CHOICES

When we were in college in the late fifties and sixties, it was assumed that a woman would study liberal arts, teaching, or nursing. A woman who studied science or engineering was really an oddball. Although some parents encouraged their daughters to get an education so that they could support themselves if they ever needed to, the real purpose of going to college was to find a husband. (Imagine the pressure this put on lesbians!) You worked after graduation only if you hadn't yet succeeded in this quest, and, of course, you quit working as soon as possible after "catching" that man. It was acceptable to put your husband through school, but then you quit. Finally, it was never okay to take a job if a married man was competing with you. *He* had the "right" to that job.

You may be saying to yourself, "Thank goodness that era is past!" If you think this description sounds dated, think again. The socialization of college women to abandon a career orientation for marriage is alive and well today. *Educated in Romance: Women, Achievement, and College Culture,* a book by anthropologists Dorothy Holland and Margaret Eisenhart, reveals that little has changed! Between 1979 and 1987, they followed the lives of young women from a predominantly white university and a predominantly black university. When these women entered college, all were good students, and about half said that they would major in science or math. Every one of them declared their intention to pursue a career after college. Yet in 1987, fewer than a third had met their own expectations. "Most had ended up with intense involvements in heterosexual romantic relationships, marginalized career identities, and inferior preparation for their likely roles as future breadwinners" (Holland and Eisenhart, 1990, p. 4).

What is disturbing about this research is not that these young women were not actively involved in a career a few years after college, but that they short-sightedly sacrificed their education and training. Few women today have the luxury of seeing work as optional. U.S. Census Bureau statistics reveal that 74 percent of women between the ages of twenty and forty now work, and it is estimated that 80 percent of the women in the United States will be in the work force by the year 2000. We have enough trouble with discrimination in the workplace without arriving there unprepared to compete.

If you think your example or teachings have protected your daughter from this trend, here's another shocker. Holland and Eisenhart found that it is the peer group, not adults, who exert pressure on young women to focus on romance to the detriment of their education. Culture changes slowly.

Being accountable involves realizing that decisions are the building blocks of a life. Major decisions—to marry, divorce, choose a career, have children, become involved in the community, or move—should be considered very carefully. Evaluate how costly a decision is (in other words, what will be lost). Remember that *not* to decide is also a decision, which may be appropriate at certain times. If the task seems overwhelming, see if you can break it down into smaller decisions; this may free you up to make the big decision. For example, I could have divorced two years earlier than I did, but I first needed to make and implement decisions that would help me become independent and self-sustaining, rather than a victim.

Lifetime Lessons in Responsibility

A young professional was rising quickly in her career—until she was introduced to cocaine. Just as quickly, she lost her job, her savings, her friendships, and her self-respect. Bereft, she returned to her parents' home on the

Payoffs for Accountability

▶ You can look in the mirror and claim your soul as your own.

▶ You can move beyond your comfort zone and increase your capacities. As Cicely Tyson said, "Challenges make you discover things about yourself that you never really knew. They're what make the instrument stretch—what make you go beyond the norm" (*The Quotable Woman*, 1991, p. 93).

▶ You can look the negative side of life squarely in the eye and not be intimidated because you know that being authentic makes it worthwhile to endure the pain.

East Coast. While they supported her, she worked as a clerk in a small store to save money for a fresh start. In the year or so it took her to get back on her feet, she had many hours to contemplate where she had gone wrong and what she needed to do differently. She realized that the key to making real change was to take charge of her life, instead of reacting passively to whatever was put in front of her. She decided to return to the same city and create a very different kind of life.

She began by staying away from any situations in which drugs would be offered to her. She formed new friendships. She set a series of specific career goals and began anew in her field. When she found herself working compulsively and thinking about drugs more and more often, she went into psychotherapy to address the self-esteem issues that drove all her compulsive behaviors. She worked less, but as her psychotherapist, Carolyn was not particularly optimistic about the likelihood that she would really change. Happily, she was wrong.

Over the years, this woman has periodically come in for therapy. She surmounts each new obstacle and then attacks the one that hides behind it. "Throughout this time," says Carolyn, "she has steadfastly stuck to her commitment to take responsibility for the form and direction of her life, and I have witnessed quite remarkable changes in every area of her life." After meeting her career goals (including getting an advanced degree and becoming vice president of a fast-growing company), she faced her fears about being in an intimate relationship with a man and came to the end of a string of heartbreaking romances. Finally, she arrived at a point where she could address the big question: "What is the meaning and purpose of my life beyond my own narrow self-interest?"

TOOLS OF EMPOWERMENT

If you set goals, you run the risk of getting what you ask for. Marilyn Taylor set a goal at the age of twenty-five: to be a vice president of a major public utility by the age of forty-five. She vowed to make the fact that she is African American and a woman assets rather than liabilities in this quest. At forty-six, she became the first black woman vice president of the Public Service Company of Colorado. Marilyn regularly writes short-term, five-year, and ten-year goals. She carries them with her in her appointment book and periodically reviews them and checks them off. This powerful woman says, "There is something about writing goals down that works. I can't honestly say that I have ever written a goal that I haven't accomplished."

Exercise   *SETTING GOALS*

The most important thing about setting goals is that you do it. It is not nearly so important to do it *right*. Set aside some time alone to go through the following steps:

1. *Design your future.* Spend ten minutes writing everything you want to do, be, and experience between now and when

you die. Your list may include items as exotic as living in Peru and as down-to-earth as getting a master's degree. Write down everything, big and small. Think about your hopes and dreams in the following categories: *health, relationships, work/career, financial, spiritual,* and *special achievements.*

From this list, identify at least five goals that you can commit to starting next year. This doesn't mean that you will accomplish them next year, but that you will be willing to invest some time pursuing them. (You may want to use the Exploring Your Values exercise in Chapter Fourteen to help you establish your goals, as well.)

2. *Commit your goals to paper.* Write out your five goals.

   a. Begin each goal with the phrase "I choose to . . ." in order to remind yourself that you are crafting your own life as you want it to be.

   b. State your goal positively ("I choose to live an abundant and prosperous life" rather than "I want to stop living in debt"—the latter is an important step, but you need to look beyond being debt-free). Focus on the outcome, not the means.

   c. To get at the real essence of each goal, ask yourself, "Why do I want that?" The answer may take you to a new goal with greater significance or broader impact. For example, your goal may be "I choose to travel more," but the reason may emerge as "I choose to travel to exotic and unusual places to understand people of different cultures."

   d. Finally, determine how you will know if you've achieved the goal. Most goals need time frames. Exceptions include goals regarding relationships or the ongoing quality of your life, which have other markers for noting your progress (for example, creating a loving and supportive atmosphere in your family).

3. *Explore your goals.* This is an optional step that is useful if you are unsure or unclear about a given goal. Write out the following:

   a. All the reasons why you should accomplish the goal

b. All the obstacles facing you

c. All the resources you have to help you accomplish the goal

d. The values you hold that support your achieving this goal

e. The personal qualities you will need to develop or enhance to accomplish this goal

f. How your goal fits into your vision for your life

4. *Make supporting choices.* Jot down action steps that support your achieving the goal. Brainstorm all the possible choices you could make and then prioritize them.

5. *Keep your goals handy.* Written goals that are regularly visible are more likely to be accomplished than those that are not. Review your goals often and schedule time to work on them.

6. *Share your goals with others.* This is another way to increase your accountability and to make your goals more real to you.

7. *Take action!*

Remember, failure can be instructive, too. In fact, you can learn a great deal about yourself by looking at the goals you *don't* meet. Steffie says, "My original goal was to stay married. Ultimately, that goal began to violate my integrity. It no longer worked. My new goal was to leave the marriage as a whole person, rather than as a wreck. More than mere survival, I wanted a life that had integrity, vitality, and fun in it."

Exercise	*ESTABLISHING YOUR BOUNDARIES*

Women often make poor choices by believing that they must endure the unendurable. Sometimes it is extremely effective to stand up and say, "I will not be treated that way" or "I just won't do this anymore."

When you feel used and abused, take on the masculine perspective and learn to protect yourself. Men are typically better at keeping roles both clear and separate (for example, work versus home). They mark off their boundaries so that people are less likely to invade their lives. They speak up when someone intrudes. Women tend to be so concerned with preserving a relationship that they will do so at the expense of their time, money, and even self-respect or personal safety.

Look at an area of your life or a specific situation that makes you feel used and abused. It may involve doing favors you later resent, taking on someone else's work when you are too busy, getting into a sexually vulnerable situation, or doing too much for your children or elderly parents.

Ask yourself:

- Did I say no? Did I say it in terms that the other person would understand, expressing my needs clearly and unambiguously?

- Did I give out mixed messages?

- Am I unclear myself about the nature of my relationship with this person?

- Do I know how far I will go for this person?

- Did I say yes when I meant no, out of guilt, fear, confusion, pity, or lack of confidence?

- Did I say yes and change my mind afterward, but fail to go back and tell the person?

To establish your boundaries:

- Get clear with yourself about where you stand in the relationship and what your position, role, or territory is.

- Clarify who is and is not welcome to join you, and under what circumstances.

- Sort out the source of your guilt, fear, confusion, lack of self-confidence, or pity. Then do what you need to do to resolve these feelings. The solution may include bringing in a trusted, respected adviser or mediator, or going to a psychotherapist.

Remember, stating your position clearly is a way of honoring the other person. You don't have to be harsh, rude, or unkind; you can be very compassionate and loving—yet firm.

Exercise *LEARNING FROM PAST DECISIONS*

1. Think of three decisions from your past that turned out to be successes and three decisions that you feel did not work out. List them in a column. Answer the following questions as you examine each decision. This exercise was based on a values clarification exercise referenced by Sidney Simon in his book *Getting Unstuck* (Simon, 1988). This revised version of the exercise will be useful for evaluating your decision-making process, as well. A grid is provided to help you organize your answers. The grid can also be used to evaluate a decision you are *currently* facing.

   a. Did you consider possible consequences? Did you investigate other options before deciding? Did you weigh the pros and cons? Did you consider how your decision would affect your relationships with others?

	SIX PAST DECISIONS	CONSIDERED PROS & CONS	INTUITION	DECIDED FREELY	CHERISHED	TOOK ACTION	BECAUSE I AM WHO I AM
SUCCESSFUL							
UNSUCCESSFUL							
	CURRENT DECISION						

b. Did you listen to your inner voice? Did you listen to your heart and follow your intuition?

c. Did you decide freely? Did you make the decision that was best for you without giving in to pressure from others?

d. Were you proud of your decision and willing to defend it when challenged? Did you share your decision with others?

e. Did you act on your decision?

f. Did you feel you had to take action because you are who you are?

2. Write out the answers to the following questions:

a. Did your successes differ from your failures? In what way?

b. Are there any decision-making steps that you need to strengthen or add?

c. What values did you identify as a result of doing this exercise?

Being accountable means being honest about your true nature and setting goals that support your authentic self. It also means taking responsibility for caring for yourself and setting limits on the demands that you place on yourself as well as those that others place on you. Finally, it requires the courage to make decisions thoughtfully and consciously, as part of a self-determined approach to life's changing demands.

12

Contentment:

EXPERIENCING LOVE AND JOY

❚❚Human felicity is produced not so much by great pieces of good fortune that seldom happen as by little advantages that occur every day.❚❚

—**Benjamin Franklin**

❚❚Believing in our hearts that who we are is enough is the key to a more satisfying and balanced life.❚❚

—**Ellen Sue Stern**

❚❚We can do no great things—only small things with great love.❚❚

—**Mother Teresa**

A FEW DAYS AFTER MY DAUGHTER was seriously injured in an automobile accident, she had the first of several surgeries. The following day, the surgeon insisted that she begin physical therapy, before her muscles stiffened up. I was sitting at her bedside when the physical therapist came into the room. When he spied this tiny, fluffy, feminine thing in the bed, he rolled his eyes, sure that she lacked the physical and emotional strength to do what he had to insist that she do. To me, he said, "I have to make her sit up and then walk. It's the only way she'll heal. I want you to wait outside. You will hear screams, but don't come back in the room, no matter what."

Oh, what agony for a mother! To see your child in pain and to be prevented from easing it—can anything be worse? After about five minutes of silence, the door opened. Several people were standing in the hallway, including staff and visitors of other patients. Amy rose up in her walker, arduously making her way forward, inch by inch. She was totally focused on executing each tiny movement. Everyone watching burst into spontaneous tears of joy. Although her face was laced with cuts and her hair was plastered to her head with blood and vomit, someone whispered, "Look! Isn't she beautiful?" Her appearance was completely transformed by her pure determination and single-minded focus as she reached into the depths of her being to summon the force to move. At that moment, I recognized the joy that can exist in any situation, no matter how terrible or sad it may be.

—*Carolyn*

JOY AMID PAIN

A constant, daily experience of love and joy is our right as human beings. It is also *possible*. It is the "glue" that holds everything together. Without it, life is dry, empty, and void of meaning, no matter how many accomplishments we have to our credit or how many possessions grace our homes. The experience of love and joy is one of contentment, gratitude, and sweetness. It flows from a sense of the completeness and perfection that exist in the moment—even in the worst of times.

Consider this recollection from concentration camp survivor Viktor Frankl:

> We stumbled on in the darkness, over big stones and through large puddles. . . . The accompanying guards kept shouting at us and driving us with the butts of their rifles. Anyone with very sore feet supported himself on his neighbor's arm. Hardly a word was spoken; the icy wind did not encourage talk. Hiding his mouth behind his upturned collar, the man marching next to me whispered suddenly: "If our wives could see us now! . . ."
>
> That brought thoughts of my own wife to mind. And as we stumbled on for miles, slipping on icy spots, supporting each other time and again, dragging one another up and onward, nothing was said, but we both knew: each of us was thinking of his wife . . . my mind clung to my wife's image, imagining it with uncanny acuteness. I heard her answering me, saw her smile, her frank and encouraging look. Real or not, her look was then more luminous than the sun which was beginning to rise.
>
> . . . Then I grasped the meaning of the greatest secret that human poetry and human thought and belief have to impart: *The salvation of man is through love and in love.* I understood how a man who has nothing left in this world may still know bliss, be it only for a brief moment, in the contemplation of his beloved. In a position of utter desolation, when man cannot express himself in positive action, when his only achievement may consist in enduring his sufferings in the right way—an honorable way—in such a position man can, through loving contemplation of the image he carries of his beloved, achieve fulfillment. (Frankl, 1959, pp. 56–57)

THE CURRENCY OF LOVE

Love is not given to us by someone else. It is not a reward for being "good." Love springs from the inner spirit and grows as we express it in our lives at every opportunity. I remember one of our children coming home from preschool joyfully singing a little song she had just learned, and the refrain still sticks in my mind: "Love is like a magic penny. If you don't give it away, you don't get any!" It's paradoxical but true. Love only grows if we constantly give it to others. What a great thing to learn at an early age! What's more, love is available all the time. Connecting with it is as easy as dipping your hand in a river as you float along in a rowboat. You don't need time to fit love into your life; it's merely a matter of reaching out and touching it as you go through your day.

BEYOND MYOPIA

Reality is a pastiche of good and bad things existing side by side. If you insist on focusing only on the misery and pain— *or* only on the joy and fulfillment—you don't see the whole picture or learn all the lessons life has to teach you. Having joy in your life is not about denying pain—it's about moving beyond it. Our culture has perpetrated a fallacy: that if we are doing things right, we can be happy all the time. In fact, life is a saga. Joy and suffering come and go. We learn from bliss *and* pain.

Once, a friend reported that several thousand dollars' worth of inventory had been stolen from the business she owned. As she shared this devastating news, her eyes widened with fear, yet she forced a broad smile and said, "I know I *should* see this as a wonderful opportunity." But it just didn't ring true. Denying your true feelings about a negative reality with a Pollyanna outlook is no more helpful than being an inveterate pessimist.

On the other hand, loving feelings give rise to more loving feelings. The more you experience flashes of love and joy, the deeper into those feelings you go, and the more readily and frequently you can tap into them. So it pays to practice doing things that bring on that experience.

> ## Payoffs for Contentment
>
> ▶ **What you do has new meaning and importance.**
>
> ▶ **You have more energy.**
>
> ▶ **A positive, hopeful attitude returns to you in difficult times.**
>
> ▶ **Life is more fun.**
>
> ▶ **Your heart opens.**
>
> ▶ **The most ordinary event can give you a lift.**

A Sense of Wonder

A woman at our meditation center has a truly radiant face. Gina Truex is an artist with a master of fine arts' degree. She is the senior designer for a firm that makes giftware. The company's products are distributed throughout the world and the business does fifteen million dollars in sales a year. In addition to her design work, Gina travels to Europe, Asia, and South America to supervise production and set quality standards for the manufacture of the products.

Recently a ten-year-old boy said to Gina, "I'd like to tell you something. I've been watching you when I come here every week. I've noticed that you're always smiling and I want you to know that it makes everyone around you feel good." It's true—everyone loves to be around her.

We asked Gina what she does that brings her such constant love and joy. She immediately replied, "I think that basically it's because I've never stopped marveling at things! It begins as soon as the sun rises. I get up early every morning so I can see it. I'm always thrilled that it is so consistently beautiful. Now I'm getting up even earlier because the stars are so brilliant and clear!

"The variety in the universe is incredible! This includes all the different people I see—even the ones who are arguing with me. As an artist I am astounded at God's creativity. He doesn't make things static. They're constantly changing—like a tree in all its different phases. And with each marvel comes a constant experience of gratitude and a sense of contentment with everything just as it is."

TOOLS OF EMPOWERMENT

Exercise   *MEDITATION*

There is a simple, age-old technique you can use to clear your mind and create the space for love and joy to emerge. We use this process in our training programs and it is wonderful to watch the transformation in people's faces and bodies in only five minutes. Women who have never meditated, or even sat still for a few minutes, are amazed at the peace and calm that comes over them and the way their spirits are lifted.

You can follow this process for a few minutes or up to an hour at a time, every day. Just as it is important to eat, drink, and rest on a regular basis, it is important to routinely focus and clear your mind. Start with whatever period of time feels good to you. You will probably find yourself wanting to increase the length of time as you become accustomed to the process. It is good to meditate first thing in the morning, late in the afternoon, or just before bed. You can also take a break for a few minutes to revive yourself at any time of the day. *To learn this process, it is helpful to have someone read the instructions to you a few times.* Set a timer for the length of time you have chosen. You might start with ten or fifteen minutes.

Find a quiet, peaceful place where you will be undisturbed by people or pets. Choose a place you find pleasing, where you are safe and warm. It may be indoors or outdoors. Pick a place you can keep coming back to, one that evokes a feeling of quiet repose.

Start by sitting in a comfortable, open, upright position. You can either sit cross-legged on the floor or ground or on a chair with your legs uncrossed, the soles of your feet flat on the floor. If you are on the floor, sitting on a cushion or blanket may make you more comfortable. Your spine should be straight, but not rigid. Your head should rest lightly on the top of your spine so that you can turn it easily from side to side. No slumping over! Make sure your chin is neither dropped forward nor tilted upward. This posture allows the breath to flow easily. Imagine a column of light flowing up from the base of your spine and out the top of your head in a straight, unobstructed line.

Let your hands rest lightly, cupped together, in your lap, or place one on each thigh. Then gently close your eyes. If they open, just close them again, until your lids relax and stay closed on their own. Check your body for any tension and simply let it go.

Take a deep breath. Breathe all the way in, filling your lungs completely. Then let it out, emptying your lungs all the way. Do this three times: Breathe in deep; breathe out long. Then let the breath return to a normal rate and watch each breath as it comes in and goes out. Let your attention become absorbed in the movement of the breath, letting go of any thoughts and feelings that may arise. Don't worry about distractions; just keep bringing your attention back to the movement of the breath.

Notice the space between breaths. There is a pause, a quiet, peaceful space between the in-breath and the out-breath. Focus on that space, continuing to let go of any distractions that arise. Let your attention become absorbed in that space more and more with each breath. Continue this process until your timer rings. You may drop into a place so still that you aren't even aware of the breath anymore; that's fine. Or thoughts may pop into your mind the entire time. That's fine too; just keep bringing your attention back to the breath, and simply watch the thoughts come and go.

When the timer rings, slowly bring your attention back to the surrounding environment. Notice any sounds in the room, then open your eyes when you are ready. Sit quietly for a moment. Be aware of your state; let it be. Then stretch, and move on to whatever is next for you.

This is also a very relaxing way to go to sleep at night. Lie on your back with your arms and legs uncrossed, and follow the process until you drift into sleep.

Tremendous benefit comes from switching from a "doing" orientation to a "being" orientation. This is difficult in our culture, which places a high value on action. Yet it is when you are living in the moment that you are able to experience its completeness and perfection. When you stop and focus utterly on the present, sweetness and joy rush in to fill the vacuum.

Exercise   *COUNT YOUR BLESSINGS*

Start or end the day by sitting quietly and thinking about all the good in your life, all the people you love. During the day, notice the things that you are grateful for; really appreciate them. Stage celebrations to share happy times with others. Doing so heightens the experience of joy and love.

Exercise   *SEEK OUT THE JOYFUL*

Discover the experiences that trigger joyful feelings for you. These can be very individual. One friend loves to go to the park. Another opens the window to listen to the sounds of children playing on the playground outside. For Carolyn, looking at the sky and watching the shifting clouds always lifts her spirits. She says, "It stops the chatter of my mind and opens me up to the beauty of the moment."

Your mind can distract and pull you away from experiencing love and joy, or you can use its power to bring you closer. You can alter your frame of reference merely by remembering an amusing or moving incident and reexperiencing the feeling. You can even close your eyes and see the face of someone you care for deeply. The feeling of love that wells up in you remains with you vividly even after you drop the image of the face. This is because the image, and the particular individual, are only triggers for the feeling, which resides within you.

Cultivating a loving, peaceful nature is an act of generosity toward yourself and others. When you seek out and embrace the joyful, beautiful aspects of life, each moment provides a new opportunity for learning and fulfillment.

13

Graciousness:

BEING COMFORTABLE TO BE AROUND

❚❚ *When she had passed, it seemed like the ceasing of exquisite music.* **❚❚**

> **—Henry Wadsworth Longfellow**

❚❚ *One of the things about equality is not just that you be treated equally to a man, but that you treat yourself equally to the way you treat a man.* **❚❚**

> **—Marlo Thomas**

❚❚ *She openeth her mouth with wisdom; and in her tongue is the law of kindness.* **❚❚**

> **—Proverbs 31:26**

*A*FTER A DAY OF TOURING AND SHOPPING in Bombay, India, my hostess entreated me to stop for a cold drink at an ice cream shop. I was exhausted from a day spent absorbing a foreign culture and maneuvering through noisy, crowded streets in the heat. I just wanted to go back to the hotel with my husband where I could be myself and relax. Yet there was a puzzling urgency in my companion's request that made me give in.

This delightful Indian woman who had been asked to escort me around was many years my senior and the wife of a prominent businessman. I had met her for the first time that morning and I was very nervous about doing or saying something insulting out of cultural ignorance. I was young and new to India, and feeling very much out of my element. All day long, I had tuned in to everything around me to try to pick up clues about Indian customs and mores. I desperately wanted to avoid being an "ugly American." I searched for topics that would be meaningful to both of us, paid attention to what my hostess found funny, and ultimately gave up being the perfect guest and simply enjoyed her company. By the time we settled into our chairs at the ice cream shop, we felt at home with each other.

As soon as our mango sodas were served, she began talking to me about her marital problems, asking me for guidance. I was astounded that she would confide in me— a young woman from a different culture with little experience as a psychologist. I struggled to respond appropriately. Mostly I asked questions and ventured my misgivings about my ability to be of help to her. I learned something valuable from her response. She told me that she felt comfortable with me, and free to be herself. She emphasized that this opportunity to be herself was in itself valuable, no matter what "expert" advice I might or might not be able to provide.

Since that time, I've thought about what makes a person comfortable to be around. (The term we have chosen for this quality is *graciousness*; although to some people the word may connote an "old-world" brand of femininity, to us it is the most accurate way to capsulize the concept as we define it.) The key seems to be to connect with others in a way that allows them to feel at ease with *themselves*. This quality springs from having a genuine interest in people and caring about them. Curiosity alone can make another person feel like a bug under a microscope, but a heartfelt interest involves appreciation, respect, and enjoyment of that particular individual.

Some people seem to have an automatic unself-conscious ability to make people comfortable. Our father was like that. He was interested in everyone he met and could always find common ground with someone, no matter what kind of cultural, educational, or racial gulf separated them. He thoroughly enjoyed people.

—Carolyn

A Pact of Trust

Graciousness also involves being trustworthy—that is, being someone who won't violate a confidence or take advantage of what others say or do when their guard is down. People pick up this kind of information about you pretty quickly. Those of us who have not developed this ability need to begin to appreciate and cultivate this capacity to make others comfortable. Even those who discover that people are readily drawn to them may find themselves in situations where that natural ability isn't enough. Thus, we all need to know what it takes to make others comfortable.

When I was in India that first time, it was important that I put a deliberate, self-conscious effort into trying to appreciate my new friend as an individual and also in the context of her culture. Once the connection had been made, I could relax and be more spontaneous. At that point, it was also important that I be myself; being at ease with ourselves is part of what makes others comfortable. We all know that pretensions or even self-consciousness make people uncomfortable and soon drive them away.

This approach allows a relationship to develop quickly and to last. When I saw my Indian friend ten years later, we both quickly settled into a comfortable place with each other. We didn't need to start over again.

THE CHAMELEON TRAP

When we talk to men and women, they tend to define being comfortable differently. Men tell us that a woman who is comfortable to be around "thinks like a man"—in other words, she is articulate, direct, and logical and can use data effectively. Most men prefer that a woman not start off by sharing her personal life; instead, they like to discuss tasks, achievements, or sports activities. Men say that they appreciate women who understand confidentiality, who let them be who they are, who know "when to speak up and when to shut up." This makes them feel at ease. They are most comfortable around women who are emotionally disciplined and calm, who are competent in their particular role in life or work, who are at ease with their own femininity, and who can take a joke—without overreacting. Although men admire strong women, they are afraid of tough women. They like women who can play hardball on their team, but not against them. They are comfortable around women who, while being straightforward and efficient, allow them to access and express their own feminine side without realizing it.

Women tend to define being comfortable quite differently. For them, a woman who is comfortable to be around is someone who doesn't put herself above them, but who connects with them at their level, whatever that level is. Women are inclined to admire a woman whose whole personality is evident, regardless of the particular role she is playing. They like a woman who downplays, rather than boasts about, her achievements in order to establish a feeling of equality. A woman who shares personal experiences and keeps her word is highly valued. Personal sharing is a sign of friendship; it is important that a woman talk about her relationships and her philosophy concerning people. She must couch criticisms carefully. While men prefer a woman who calls a spade a spade, women like women who put a rosy tint on things. We find that most women feel comfortable around a woman who relies on group process to solve problems and who takes time to build consensus.

Since in many ways these two pictures are antithetical, the empowered woman is often forced to make choices. In mixed-gender groups, when there are time constraints for getting a job done, she may have to put her relationships with women at risk, or work on building them behind the scenes. Remember, if your vision and goals are clearly identified, you will know where to take a stand and where to take risks. The ultimate solution is to be yourself. That authenticity, more than anything else, will make others comfortable with you, because it allows them to express *their* uniqueness.

We typically think of authenticity in terms of being spontaneous. However, being yourself may include knowing how your personal interactions with men or women typically get off track and developing some strategies for behaving differently at certain times. For example, Carolyn says, "My forthrightness is admired by men, but I now realize that it makes women uncomfortable. So if I see a woman pulling back, I check to see if I need to soften my message a bit."

Charm in the Executive Suite

Barbara Grogan, president of an industrial construction company, is the chair of the Greater Denver Chamber of Commerce. Recently Steffie visited her office to ask her for some help with a project she was working on. Steffie recalls, "Rather than greeting me in her office suite, she came down to the reception desk to meet me. She suggested that we go to the conference room to chat and stopped to get us some coffee on the way.

"She immediately engaged me by asking me how I was doing and what some of the interesting challenges in my life were. Her manner made me want to divulge things to her. After I outlined what I wanted, she enthusiastically gave me names of people I should talk to and offered to call them first to help set up meetings for me. The next time I saw her, it was as though we'd had a ten-minute break. She remembered our connections and asked me what else she could do for me. Barbara was utterly gracious and generous with her

Payoffs for Graciousness

▶ **Both men and women want to work with you.**

▶ **Because excellence is voluntary, you're more likely to get excellent work from others.**

▶ **People are more honest and willing to share information and ideas with you.**

▶ **You attract a greater variety of people and thus build more effective teams.**

▶ **You waste less time dealing with tensions and conflicts.**

time and energy. The entire time I was with her, I felt that she was totally focused on me, and totally *present*. I never felt hurried. Her smile and twinkling eyes revealed her enthusiasm and connectedness, as she worked to find solutions to my needs."

TOOLS OF EMPOWERMENT

Exercise   *BROADENING YOUR MIND*

In the interest of cultivating a comfortable manner, it is to your advantage to develop a genuine liking for many kinds of people. This is a skill that can be learned. You can practice in places where many diverse individuals congregate, such as a busy downtown street or the airport. As you watch the people around you, identify things you like about them. Then go on to do the same thing with your work group. Finally, probe deeper. Ask yourself, "What else might I like about these people if I gave them half a chance?"

Here is another approach to try. Think about people whom you greatly admire and write down the qualities you like in them. See if you can find those qualities in more people in your circle.

Next, focus on people you don't like because they make you uncomfortable. It may be because of your own biases. Try to figure out why they bother you. Is it their appearance? Their social class? Their ethics? Do they frighten you? Then open-mindedly work to rid yourself of your limiting beliefs about them. Consider the following points:

- Appearance is only packaging. Carolyn shares an experience. "One day, I was frowning at some outrageously dressed 'punker' teenagers when my teenaged daughter said, 'Think of them as tropical fish, Mom.' This was such a wonderful image! I immediately smiled and the kids dropped their tough facades and smiled back. I remembered that they were teenagers, just like my own child, and no doubt had many likeable qualities. So I think about tropical fish when I find myself giving a disapproving look, and remind myself to look past appearances to the beings within."

- Manners and class are likewise simply your preferred way of doing things, and not necessarily "correct." Becoming comfortable means learning to accept a diversity of backgrounds and behaviors. Carolyn says, "My husband's family background is very different from mine. The summer I visited them for the first time, we had a friend who was leading a group to live with Indians in the Andes Mountains. My husband said, 'I'm taking *you* on a trip to a different culture, too!' With this mindset, I learned to appreciate their way of life, to participate in it where it felt 'right,' and to just enjoy it where it didn't."

- If another person's ethics directly affect you (causing you a loss of time, money, or work performance, for example), it can be a source of discomfort for both of you. It is important to recognize this conflict and get it out in the open. Acknowledging your differences helps improve the situation and makes you more comfortable—and more comfortable to be around.

- If you dislike someone because he or she makes you fearful, examine *why*. There could be a very realistic cause for concern. To exercise your discrimination, ask yourself what the worst-case scenario would be involving this person's trait. If your fear is realistic, develop a plan of action to get yourself out of danger. If not, drop it.

Exercise *TUNING IN TO OTHERS*

Many people feel that consciously modifying their behavior to make others more comfortable smacks of manipulation. We believe that it is no different from speaking in terms that other people will understand, tailoring the message to the listener. Consider case studies done in the field of Neuro-Linguistic Programming. Researchers tracked the behavior of therapists who stood out as being "gifted" or especially adept at connecting with their clients. It turned out that these professionals used *pacing* and *leading*. Early on in their encounters, they would *pace* their clients, matching their body language and rate and tone of speech, in effect joining them. Then they would uncross their arms, relax, and speak more quickly, beginning to move in their own direction— *leading* their clients. The clients in these instances were more receptive and less likely to resist during the conversation because the therapists had first joined them at their emotional level (Grindler and Bandler, 1981). These are skills you can practice to help others to be more comfortable around you.

Exercise *LISTENING*

Here is a place to practice both *active listening* and *deep listening*. In active listening, you respond spontaneously to what the other person is saying. You may indicate your agreement or share your own experience as a way of letting the other person know you hear and understand what is being said. Look for elements you have in common. Share your feelings and opinions readily, but check frequently to see that you are not distorting what the other person is telling you. Deep listening is described in Chapter Six. When you are engaged in deep listening, you put aside your personal reactions and simply absorb what the other person is saying, as well as who he or she is. Explaining that you are trying to fully understand what your companion is communicating will help that person to understand why you might be quiet or look away to focus more fully on what is being said.

Exercise   *TRUSTING*

Train yourself to be willing to give others the benefit of the doubt. Unless you have a strong reason not to trust someone, put aside your initial negative reactions and allow yourself to wait and see what develops. You may be taken in now and then, but it is better to be conned occasionally than never to be duped at the price of being closed off and cold-hearted!

Exercise   *MAKING MEN COMFORTABLE*

The following is a list of behaviors that you can practice to make men more comfortable with you. Doing so enhances your versatility by adding to your repertoire. This doesn't mean turning yourself into a man! Choose from or add to the list provided below. Then the next time you are in a mostly male environment, consciously practice the behaviors you have selected.

- Speak directly to the point, rather than being manipulative.
- Don't let emotions undermine what you have to say.
- State the result you seek.
- Be prepared with factual data.
- Dress appropriately so as not to detract from credibility.
- Honor a challenged response—listen, and don't become defensive.
- Use humor to lighten the tone.
- Separate personal and business matters.
- Focus on the task you are sharing.
- Find subtle ways to establish your competence.
- Be consistent.

Exercise   *MAKING WOMEN COMFORTABLE*

From the following list, select behaviors to practice in order to make women feel more comfortable around you. Add any others you may think of.

- Spend some time with people you don't normally talk to.
- Share a funny anecdote about yourself that connects you to them.
- Think of three or four positive things to tell the group.
- Look for possible areas for collaboration.
- Negotiate.
- Suggest, rather than command.
- Give and receive help.
- Seek consensus.
- Consider group members' feelings.
- Point out what is going right.
- Show respect for group members.
- Be flexible.

A truly gracious woman can be riveting. She inspires confidence, fosters cooperation, and fairly sparkles with self-possessed femininity. Others seek her out, eager to spend time in her soothing company.

14

Alignment:

ALIGNING YOUR THOUGHTS, FEELINGS, ACTIONS, AND VALUES

❚❚ *There is only one success—to be able to live your life in your own way.* **❚❚**
—Christopher Morley

❚❚ *You cannot drive straight on a twisting lane.* **❚❚**
—Russian proverb

❚❚ *To be nobody-but-myself—in a world which is doing its best, night and day, to make you everybody else—means to fight the hardest battle which any human being can fight, and never stop fighting.* **❚❚**
—E. E. Cummings

S EVERAL YEARS AGO, I WAS ASKED TO SERVE on the board of a newly formed nonprofit organization for recovering alcoholics. Initially, I felt flattered and excited at the prospect. The organization offered an innovative approach to assisting alcoholics to find meaningful work once they had left the hospital. The executive director was brilliant and inspirational, like a wonderful hybrid of Albert Schweitzer and Peter Pan, and I enjoyed all the board members I had met. I also knew that I had the skills to be of service to the board.

Yet I was uncomfortable. I found myself reluctant to commit to the position in spite of being genuinely supportive of the organization and the people in it. To gain perspective, I discussed my feelings with my brother-in-law. In the process, I discovered that the work I was contemplating didn't feel right, wasn't consistent with my values, and was out of alignment with my vision, which had to do with men and women working together effectively. Although the work was very worthwhile, I saw that I placed a higher priority on helping other groups of people. In the end, I declined the board position and felt relieved to have done so. Over the years since this experience, I have learned to listen to my intuitions about what feels "right" for me, in order to make sure that the commitments I make are consistent with who I am and what I hold dear.

—Steffie

LINKING HEAD, HEART, AND FEET

Alignment is central to empowerment. It is a recurring theme in the lives of effective leaders. Being aligned means that what you think, feel, and do are in sync. This flows out of a sense of "rightness" within you. As a result, your actions gain power, and others are drawn to you.

To visualize alignment, think of yourself as a human being whose head, heart, and feet are all in a line, facing in the same direction. When you are angry, you are angry. When you are glad, you are glad. You feel it and everyone else can see it because your behavior is sending congruent messages. On the other hand, when you are out of alignment, you feel scattered, unfocused, and out of whack, as if every part of you were going in a different direction. Others are confused by your behavior or are inclined to read into it what they want to see.

The most effective way to achieve alignment is by consciously striving to understand your highest values. These values are the underpinning for everything you think, feel, and do. For the purposes of this chapter, we define a value as the primary reason you do what you do. Values are not casual preferences, but deep motivations. Some examples might be "continuous intellectual growth," "a close-knit family," and "total honesty."

VALUES TEST

To act with integrity, we must act on our values. In this way, what we think, feel, and do will be in alignment, and our lives will have congruence. You can apply the following tests to see whether your behavior is in alignment with your values and to clarify what values are involved:

- If some course of action will violate your values, you will find yourself saying, "In this situation, at this time, *I can't do that and be me.*" Then ask yourself, "What values will I violate if I follow that course of action?"

- Likewise, when you feel compelled to do something that expresses your values, you will say, "In this situation, at this time, *I must do that because of who I am.*" Then ask yourself, "What values will I be acting on here?"

The qualifier "In this situation, at this time . . ." acknowledges the fact that different values rule in different circumstances.

Everyone has values. They are acquired from your culture, the era in which you live, your family, and your experiences in life. At key times in your life, you consciously reject, adopt, or modify the values you have been handed. This is a normal and essential part of maturation.

We are who we are today in large part because of all the choices we have made up to this point. Values enter into our choices, decisions, and actions. Understanding the connection between values and actions is the key to acting more consistently and with greater conviction. It is not an easy process, but the rewards are great.

HOW ALIGNMENT IS DERAILED

The following are some pitfalls to avoid:

- *Chewing endlessly on internal conflicts.* Replaying conversations over and over in your mind is a dead-end activity. Resolve these conflicts by talking them through with someone else or writing about them in your journal until clarity comes. Resolution of a major, ongoing unresolved conflict may require psychotherapy. Find help and stop putting it off!

- *Clinging to the past.* Realize that your values do change and shift as you grow, and that where you put your energy also changes all the time. Accept the change and flux of life and the constant process of reexamination and realignment that goes along with it.

- *Putting others' needs first.* Or you may seesaw between putting others' needs first and indulging your own whims, then feel guilty for both! Remember to consider who you are as an individual as you decide where to spend your time. Think about what *you* value and see that your life reflects those values. Listen to your own heart.

A Midlife Realignment

Kay Johnson was one of the original founding partners of The Athena Group. In the early stages of creating the

Payoffs for Alignment

▶ You make better decisions, rather than self-defeating choices.

▶ You feel that you are focused, rather than scattered.

▶ You find it easier to say no to things that don't fit your life.

▶ You manage your time better.

▶ You have greater chances for fulfillment and less inner conflict and struggle.

▶ You have a basis for "cleaning house" to create greater harmony in your everyday life.

business, she found the work tremendously challenging and stimulating. The opportunity to make a difference in the lives of many women excited her. After a few years with the company, however, she grew vaguely dissatisfied. While training participants in empowerment classes, she found herself unable to complete the visioning exercises that the participants were doing. She began to notice an incongruity between what she was teaching and what was true in her own life. At the same time, the routine problems and challenges of the business began to seem overwhelming and insur-mountable. Gradually, her commitment to her daily work began to wane.

These growing feelings of unease came to a head when Kay attended her thirtieth high school reunion. During a tour of the high school, she stayed behind the group and walked out on the stage of the auditorium where she had first performed to a large audience, and where she had decided that she wanted to be a singer. At that moment, she was overcome with emotion. As she describes the experience, it was not nostalgia for past triumphs that she felt, but a deep, persistent longing. Into the dark, empty auditorium, she said aloud, "What is this *about?*" Upon reflection, she recalled that the high points of her life had involved participating in theater and music. Why, she wondered, had she been unable to allow herself to pursue this passion fully?

Several weeks later, she was introduced as "the embodiment of an empowered woman" when she gave a speech to a group of women. She cringed inwardly, thinking to herself, "Not by *our* definition—I'm not doing what I care about most."

She realized that she had been distracted throughout her life by what others thought and expected of her. What complicated things further was that the crisis wasn't an acute one, because she had always managed to find experiences that were in large measure satisfying, pursuits that allowed her to learn and to grow intellectually. Thoughts like these swam in her mind, absorbing her. After an agonizing six months of soul searching, Kay told us, her partners, that she wanted to leave the company in order to pursue her artistic vision. In spite of the uncertainty she feels about exactly how she will manifest her vision for her life, making the decision to pursue it has given her a greater sense of alignment. She is convinced that she has reconnected with her true path in life.

TOOLS OF EMPOWERMENT

Exercise   *EXPLORING YOUR VALUES*

1. Make a list of twenty things you love to do. These can be major or minor activities, things you have always done or things you have just begun to do. Be specific. Then jot down the answers to the following questions beside each item.

    a. Is this something you do alone, or with others?

    b. Is this an activity that you would like to become better at?

c. Is this something you would like to do more often?

d. Is it a new interest, or a long-held one?

e. How recently have you engaged in this activity?

f. Is this something you are praised or validated for by others?

g. Reviewing the list, which five are the most important to you? Rank order them from 1 to 5.

In looking at the activities you love the most, consider what values are revealed in each one. For example, one of Steffie's favorite activities is reading. Underlying her love of reading are the values of constantly learning new things, exploring the unknown, gaining historical knowledge, and enhancing her self-knowledge. Be sure to refer back to this list when you are setting your goals in Chapter Eleven.

2. Look at yourself through objective eyes. Walk through your house as if you were looking at the house of someone you didn't know. List the values that are revealed by the things you have placed in your home.

3. Scrutinize your appointment book. Does the way you spend your time reflect your important values, or does it show that you are out of alignment?

| Exercise | *RESOLVING AN INTERNAL-VALUES CONFLICT* |

What can you do when your highest values come into conflict? The classic example is that of the woman whose presence is required at a critical business meeting on a morning when her child, aging parent, or close friend is sick. She values being professional and keeping her work commitments *and* she values supporting those who are dear to her, especially when they are helpless and frightened. Clearly, there are no "right" answers, but if you can isolate your values, you have a better basis for making a decision. (Note: For an exercise dealing with an external-values conflict, see Chapter Fifteen.)

1. Select a decision you are currently trying to make that involves conflicting values. (If you've resisted making the

decision for some time, warring values within you may well be the cause of your indecision.) Write out as many answers to the following questions related to that decision as you can. Then do the same thing for the alternative:

a. I need to _____ because _____ .

b. I want to _____ because _____ .

c. But _____ .

2. Next, try to identify the values represented in what you have written about both alternatives. Ask yourself:

a. Which choice best reflects my highest value at this moment?

b. Which choice most honors my integrity?

c. What price will I pay for acting on that value? Am I willing to pay the price?

d. My next step to resolve this conflict will be _____ .

Living in alignment is a way of conserving emotional and physical energy. It requires constant truthfulness with oneself and regular self-scrutiny, but it yields vast amounts of satisfaction and inner peace.

15

Communication:

COMMUNICATING WELL
WITH OTHERS

❚❚Human speech is like a cracked kettle on which we tap crude rhythms for bears to dance to, while we long to make music that will melt the stars.**❚❚**

—**Gustave Flaubert**

❚❚Good communication is stimulating as black coffee, and just as hard to sleep after.**❚❚**

—**Anne Morrow Lindbergh**

❚❚Eloquence: saying the proper thing and stopping.**❚❚**

—**Stanley Link**

*I*N THE MIDDLE OF A JOINT BUSINESS VENTURE with a growing company, I grew frustrated with my key contact person. Although he was a professional, creative, ethical man, he was also overcommitted and swamped with work. Our project was stalled on his end.

I had tried calling him to ask what I could do to help him out, but to no avail. One day I hit on a solution. I took a purple Nerf ball and stuffed it into a small pencil case, which I wrapped with duct tape. Inside the case, I wrote the words: "The ball is in your court." I put the case in a fancy box and wrapped it in beautiful gift paper. I had the package delivered by the night watchman so it would be sitting on the man's desk when he arrived in the morning.

It worked! He called me later that day to lay out a time line for the next four months. I had found a way to gently tease his competitive nature (knowing he would want the ball to be back in *my* court). It was also more effective for me to communicate by not using words alone, and in an unusual fashion. My message and my medium created energy and fun for him rather than merely adding one more obligation to an already overloaded agenda.

—Steffie

THE COMMUNICATION PUZZLE

To most of us, the word *communication* connotes spoken language. Yet research has shown that 55 percent of what we communicate comes through our facial expressions and body language, 38 percent through our tone of voice (including virtually all interpersonal meaning), and *only 7 percent through our words* (Mehrabian, 1968, p. 53).

Our individual differences become very important in this process. Each of us has a communication style, reflected in what we choose to communicate verbally as well as in what we choose to hear. We have distinctive preferences for content that is related to facts, results, "people" information, or "pizazz"—what's exciting or interesting to us. We tend to focus the content of what we say on these areas, and also to listen for this content. Thus, we all tend to be partial senders and partial receivers, filtering what we say and hear according to our individual preferences. Good communicators are those who have learned to build a bridge between their preferences and those of others.

The communication game is further complicated by gender differences. As Deborah Tannen has documented so effectively in her book *You Just Don't Understand* (1990), men typically use language to establish status, to demonstrate their expertise, and to claim their place in the social or corporate hierarchy. As a result, they communicate to swap content and information. In the corporate world, this equates to focusing on tasks, on end results, and on the bottom line. Women, on the other hand, more often use language to create relationships, connections, and community. Once these bridges have been built, information can flow comfortably.

Men become uncomfortable when you dominate the conversation and take away their ability to demonstrate their knowledge and status. Women become uncomfortable when an exchange of personal information is circumvented in favor of "getting down to business" right off the bat. In groups of men and women together, men's communication style predominates. Not only is men's style more commanding, demanding, and domineering, but we live in a man's world, especially in the workplace. The evidence of this is all around us. Watch in meetings. You'll notice that men speak up first and then interrupt women twice as often as they interrupt other men. They are used to competing for air time and use language in an almost combative fashion; only after they have established their status relative to one another can they relax and establish community. Women, on the other hand, require that others—men or women—first establish a connection with us in order to be accepted as equals and welcomed into our community.

Here is another way in which this is played out. When women meet for the first time, we typically do not promote our achievements, credentials, or titles. Almost always, we add personal information, such as family data, into our introductions. On the other hand, men's introductions are typically a list of their credentials.

On the whole, women are better listeners than men. One reason for this is that since men dominate the conversation, women have time to listen. Women are more inclined to listen actively: to look the speaker in the eye, to nod, to smile. Men tend to be poker-faced. As listeners, men tend to sort for facts and roles. Women tend to sort for relationships, connections, and ways to collaborate.

Massaging the Message

To better communicate with men:

- Become a more complete listener. Be aware of the things you typically listen for, and expand the list. For example, if you normally are interested in information regarding relationships, discipline yourself to listen for and recall the factual data that punctuate a conversation.

- Speak out more often and in a more comfortably commanding mode. Men pay attention when you communicate something worthwhile and relevant to the task at hand that demonstrates your competence and that is delivered with confidence.

- Because women are cooperative sorts, we don't get to the point quickly enough for some men's tastes. We also have a habit of couching our statements in qualifiers, which weaken our message. Watch your use of words like "however," "maybe," "let's try," and "if possible"—they can discredit you. Also watch for directives couched as requests: "Would you mind if . . . ," "You might want to possibly try to . . . ," "If it's okay with you . . . ," and so on.

- Realize that men are often terrified of emotional women—especially angry women. A complicating factor in emotionally charged encounters is that women often automatically cry when we are angry. Learn to talk *through* the tears (refusing to be consoled) and stick to the point.

A friend who was the first woman in her school district to be appointed principal of an elementary school had constant run-ins with the school superintendent. In their meetings together, he repeatedly attacked and criticized her. She would sit there quietly trying to hold herself together until, finally, the tears began to flow. The minute she began to cry, he would end the meeting and leave the room. She was left unable to respond to anything he had said or done.

Finally, one day, she started a meeting by telling him that if she were upset, she might cry, but that she needed to be heard nonetheless, and she would continue to talk even while crying. She told him that she expected him to hear her out, as it was only fair that she get her chance to speak, since he would have had his chance. He responded to her insistence that he "play fair," although he could hardly stay in his chair the next time she began to cry. She kept right on talking as she had agreed to do, saying at one point, "You'll notice that I am rational and making sense even though I am crying!" He agreed that it was true. While he never got comfortable with any expression of emotion on her part, he tolerated it and was glad to actually finish their meetings.

Be aware that if you are dealing with a woman who has spent a long time in a man's world, she probably will have adapted to men's mode of communication and will be more impatient with "process." When you find a woman using a masculine way of communicating, play by men's rules, but keep your eyes open for a way to establish a relationship, too.

To help the men in your life talk to you more effectively, make them aware of the following differences:

- For women, the time spent asking personal questions is not frivolous chatter, but a basis for connection. Women naturally store this information as a way of connecting with others later. Men can learn to do this.

- Women take more time talking up front, because we are more comfortable once the relationship has been established. Men need to take this into account in their interactions with women and just let the chitchat go on. It's a sort of conversational foreplay.

- When men shift abruptly out of the "friendly" mode, it makes women feel manipulated. They need to preserve a congenial style throughout the interchange. The message in the sudden shift seems to be "Enough of this trivia, let's do what counts," which negates the opening exchange.

- Men should see silence as a red flag. Most of the time, women won't object to something overtly. We tend to become silent and withdraw instead. (Then, we complain about it to our friends!) Ask what's wrong.

LOOKING THE PART

First impressions last a lot longer than we want them to and count for more than we expect. Given this immutable truth, you need to learn to use your image to communicate the message you want.

Sometimes women make the mistake of dressing inappropriately because we want to be seen and known as our whole selves. For example, Steffie naturally likes to dress like a gypsy—doing so communicates her free-spirited nature. "However, I found I couldn't do this in the business world because I wasn't taken seriously," she says. "I need to dress to support my role—as a corporate executive and a company president—and confine myself to adding gypsy touches that allow me creativity and personal expression even in that conservative setting."

Assess your audience, and take into account their style and standards. Make an effort to dress like "one of them," or at least in a way that is not radically different. You want their attention to be focused on what you say and do, not riveted on what you look like—and their own discomfort with it. You may want to consider asking a friend who has the right "look," or even hiring an image consultant, to help you with your wardrobe. It may seem extravagant, but spending a few hours going through your closet with a pro can work wonders. The chances are that you are not terribly objective about what your clothes say about you and could benefit from an outsider's perspective. A consultant can help you build your wardrobe or replace it with one that is more in keeping with both your audience and your life-style.

Certainly, you have multiple images, but start with the one that suits the role you spend the most time in and work to develop that. You might want to arrange your closet according to your roles—as businesswoman, athlete, mother, and so on.

Another idea is to investigate your clients' dress code. If the company is large, walk around to get a sense of the standards there. If you don't have the opportunity to do this, a rule of thumb is to be dressed at least as well as your client as a sign of respect.

A very important reminder: Men are many times more distracted by visual images of the opposite sex than women are. Looking at women affects men in a way that is hard for us to appreciate. This doesn't mean that you should dress like a man and blend into the woodwork. Instead, you should dress to look professional, competent, and feminine without flaunting your sexuality. You don't need to worry about sacrificing your womanliness; much of your femininity can be creatively expressed through your unique choice of colors, fabrics, and styles of clothing.

Payoffs for Communication

▶ **You accomplish tasks with minimum effort.**

▶ **You are seen as competent.**

▶ **People seek you out as a mediator or facilitator in dicey situations.**

▶ **You bring more joy and less anger to the world.**

▶ **You solve "people" problems when others can't.**

A Flair for Connecting

Dottie Lamm is an expert communicator. Wife of the former governor of Colorado, book author, newspaper columnist, and national speaker, Dottie can communicate with men, women, and mixed-gender groups with ease and finesse. Naturally introverted, Dottie developed her communication skills in order to influence people, accomplish tasks, and build relationships. She has learned to align her tone of voice, appearance, and words to maximize every communication opportunity.

She builds bridges quickly, establishing a bond with shared information. The process is genuine. When she talks one-on-one with men, she speaks directly to the point with enormous graciousness and humor. Still, she doesn't let them get off the hook. Her questions can be penetrating, although she saves her demands for the issues that are most important. In mixed audiences, Dottie communicates from her head *and* heart. When delivering a speech on an issue she cares about, she marshals all of her facts, spells out and meets her objectives, and demonstrates her commitment and competence by sharing her personal experiences. Her words and tone carry the message of her genuine concern and caring. She threads humor throughout the talk, which creates a level of comfort in the audience. Finally, she inspires her listeners to take action. People come away from their encounters with Dottie feeling honored and pleased to have been around her.

TOOLS OF EMPOWERMENT

Exercise   WHAT *DID THEY SAY?*

You can discover your listening bias by pairing up with a friend or spouse. After both of you have listened to ten minutes of a movie, a dinner table conversation, or a meeting, compare notes about what you heard, and what the essential message was. It is important to try this out in varied settings (for example, work and home) because you may have been trained to extend your natural preference in a given setting. Once you have discovered what your slant is, practice listening for other things. Go outside your comfort zone.

| Exercise | *COMMUNICATING ANGER EFFECTIVELY* |

What makes getting angry so frightening is the feeling of being out of control. There are four signs that someone is angry and out of control:

1. The person attacks you.

2. The person blames you.

3. The person says yes, but doesn't mean it and sabotages you later.

4. The person avoids you (doing everything from looking away to vanishing).

Each of us has a preferred anger style and a preferred "fallback" style, which is how we behave when we are really backed against the wall. For example, if your normal response when you're angry is avoidance and you now find yourself raging at someone, it means you're *really* out of control.

The following is a tried-and-true technique for communicating your anger and getting results. It is taken from the book *People Skills: How to Assert Yourself, Listen to Others and Resolve Conflicts* by Robert Bolton, Ph.D. (1979). Rather than threatening the relationship, using this technique will actually strengthen it. The goal is to get the other person to share responsibility for solving the problem. To that end, it is important to follow the steps exactly. Keep pushing for a solution you can both live with.

1. Begin by breaking your issue down into three parts: exactly what you are angry about, how you feel, and the effects of the other person's behavior on you. Use the following model:

   "When you _____, I feel _____ because _____."

Note: The effects on you must be concrete and specific in order for this technique to work. If the conflict is an issue of values or aesthetics, you need a different approach (see the following section, "Resolving a Value Conflict with Another Person").

Here is an example of these three elements all strung together:

"When you are late to work, I feel angry
because I have to cover your job and mine
and that affects the quality of my work."

2. Write down your three-part sentence. This is important because when you deliver the message, you will need to say it verbatim, repeating it over and over until it is heard and the other person takes responsibility for action.

3. Prepare yourself for the confrontation emotionally and intellectually. Get centered. Walk around the block, do deep breathing—whatever it takes to get yourself steady and focused. Set up a time to talk to the person; allow half an hour. Tell the person what you intend to talk about—unless you're dealing with an avoider, who may flee the country! Take your written sentence with you so you can repeat it exactly. Remember, you may have to repeat it five to ten times. Understanding is *not* the same as acceptance.

4. Brace yourself for the fallout. The other person will go into a defense or attack mode, either raging at you, blaming you, ignoring you, or acquiescing, depending on his or her preferred style.

   a. If you are attacked or blamed, remain calm and unaffected. The rage will dissipate. You may want to take notes, but don't get engaged in the battle or permit the conversation to get off track.

   b. Acquiescers will appear to give in and may be apologetic, but don't let them off the hook until they take responsibility for doing something about the problem.

   c. Avoiders hate confrontation and may refuse to deal with the issue at all. You need to hunt them down and force them to be involved.

   In each case, you should repeat your message until the person begins to deal with the issue. Use his or her response to segue back into your sentence. For example, to the acquiescer, you might say, "I accept your apology, but when you are late to work, I feel angry because I have to do the work for both of us, which lowers the quality of my work."

Remember these keys to a successful confrontation:

- Deal with behavior, not values.

- Break your issue down into a clear, accurate three-part sentence.

- Deliver the sentence in a no-nonsense manner that shows the other person that you are committed to finding a solution right then and there, and that you will not let up until the other person has agreed to work with you to solve it.

This technique requires discipline, but if it is done with integrity and caring, and if you are committed enough to follow through and hang tough, you will get your issue resolved. Most of the time a confrontation undertaken in this manner will lead to a closer and more affectionate relationship than before. The chance to improve your working relationship and forge a greater bond is a powerful incentive to try this systematic approach to conflict resolution.

Exercise — RESOLVING A VALUE CONFLICT WITH ANOTHER PERSON

The approach in the preceding exercise is not a good technique for resolving value clashes. These require another approach, because you simply can't change another person's values. One way women go wrong is in thinking that if they talk long enough they can always work things out. Some issues are simply nonnegotiable.

Examples of value conflicts in a work milieu might include differences in professional work standards, levels of service given a client, the manner in which reports are delivered and presented, or how much a team is driven to meet deadlines that affect other aspects of the company.

The goal is to find common ground, and for that you must negotiate. First of all, you have to come to the meeting with an open mind and heart, and with a genuine desire to work things out. The following technique for problem solving without polarization incorporates work from Peter G. Ossorio, Ph.D., and Warren Ziegler.

1. In a spirit of goodwill invite the other person to join you in a discussion of the issue that is troubling you. Set a time and place for the discussion. Make sure you have enough time to make some progress, and the privacy needed to be candid with each other.

2. Enter into the discussion with good faith. Commit yourself to giving it your best effort. Without this condition, nothing will happen.

3. Take the stance of mutual learning. This is a basically cooperative venture where you join together in a "community of learners." Through your combined efforts you have the opportunity to create something greater than would be possible alone.

4. Treat yourself and the other person with respect.

5. Be aware of and demonstrate your appreciation for what each of you has to offer.

6. If the trust level is low, anger is high, or skills are new or undeveloped, call in a third party to keep you on track and to see that these guidelines are being followed. Make sure it is someone you both trust to be fair and impartial.

7. Both you and the other person have a chance to give your view of the situation and your position on it, an opportunity to say, "This is how I see it. This is what I think should be done."

8. As the other person speaks, practice deep listening.

9. "Be" that person as you listen. Notice the relevant facts of his or her situation. Notice what it feels like to be in the other person's situation.

10. Then reflect back to the other person what you heard and ask any questions that will help clarify your understanding of his or her view. Check to make sure that your understanding is accurate until you are both comfortable.

11. When it is your turn, speak clearly and directly. Use tact and sensitivity where they are called for.

12. Share both the facts and feelings that are important to enabling the other person to understand your position.

As you do, speak in the first person. "Own" your personal viewpoint.

13. After each of you has spoken, take turns responding to each other's position, observing all the above guidelines.

14. Next, share any changes in your own perspective that have occurred as a result of this initial exchange. Listen to the other person's new position. Share yours. Respond to each other again.

15. Continue this process until (a) a mutually shared view has emerged, allowing you to proceed to implement the solution, *or* (b) you are clear about each other's perspectives but are still in disagreement—you agree to disagree at this point and can move on to making trade-offs. This involves making trades to achieve some kind of parity ("I'll do this for you, if you'll do this for me"). This keeps the power balance even, allows each person to get something he or she wants, and allows both people to move forward. Making trades may or may not involve compromise. It does involve giving something of yourself—but not giving yourself away.

16. If you become stuck, take some time off and then get back together. Set an agreed-upon time to reconvene before you part. Sometimes you need some time or distance to think things through, or to get in touch with what is making you uncomfortable, before you can reach a resolution.

17. When your negotiation is successful, don't forget to celebrate. Go out to lunch, announce the results publicly—whatever you feel will honor the work you have done together.

Remember: A resolution is an end point that allows you to move forward in a way you couldn't before, and that does not do serious damage to either party. It is not necessarily about agreement, or happiness, or achieving a complete solution.

Exercise   *THREE QUICK TRAINING TIPS*

Finally, here are some more ideas for improving your communication:

1. Develop the skill of "deep listening" (see Chapter Six).

2. Pay attention to exactly what you want to get across and let any extraneous information fall by the wayside. This takes discipline, especially if you are talkative by nature. This strategy is just as helpful to those who feel shy and inarticulate as it is to those who are outspoken, because if you know what you want to say, the right words will come.

3. Refine your message. If your challenge has to do with your tendency to soften or dilute your message, enlist the help of a friend who will tell you when you use too many qualifying words or circle around your subject. Building your awareness in this way can help you eliminate those obstacles from your communication. If you are too direct, ask for coaching from a friend who is known for being tactful. A strong message delivered compassionately is more likely to be heard and considered.

Good communicators excel at making a complicated process look easy. When they speak, their words, body language, and facial expressions are congruent. They always check to make sure that they've been understood. And they work constantly to clarify and fine-tune their communication, by being open to receiving messages from others.

16

Versatility:

WORKING EFFECTIVELY
WITH MEN AND WOMEN

❚❚ *What is most beautiful in virile men is something feminine; what is most beautiful in feminine women is something masculine.* **❚❚**

—**Susan Sontag**

❚❚ *Make no judgments where you have no compassion.* **❚❚**

—**Anne McCaffrey**

❚❚ *Every time we liberate a woman, we liberate a man.* **❚❚**

—**Margaret Mead**

ONE OF THE TOUGHEST EXPERIENCES I EVER HAD in the predominantly male world of business occurred when I was CEO of a software company. The challenge before me was to raise money in a public stock offering. This involved creating effective, well-organized presentations for brokers and prospective investors, as well as assembling a management team that could handle being grilled on the potential and expertise of the company. I knew I had to speak "male" language and come across as decisive, factual, committed, and knowledgeable or I would never be taken seriously.

Yet during this period, I often felt motherly as I nurtured and supported my team. One employee quailed at public speaking, and I coached him through his fear. In tense times, I had to be resolute, yet always gracious. Had I become too "masculine," I would have alienated potential investors, as well as my own team.

In some ways, being a female CEO hampered me. I was frequently told that women weren't tough enough to handle the issues affecting a small business. In response to this prejudice, I had to show tremendous emotional discipline, which was difficult for a feeling person like me. This meant, among other things, not getting too involved in other people's personal problems. I couldn't show fear or uncertainty, even though I was doing many things for the very first time in my life. I also had to change some of my attitudes, for example, transforming my contempt for greed into respect for a fair profit. While maintaining a smoothly functioning organization, I had to have many knock-down-drag-out battles behind the scenes with both my own team and investors.

Throughout this experience, I encountered many decent men who were willing to help me by contributing their wisdom and perspective. At times, men's fairness helped me. I could count on it, which reassured me. And there was room in my role for a lot of affection to be shown. When the placement finally closed (meaning that we had raised enough money to make the offering fly), the company's male chief financial officer and I accepted public congratulations; then we closed the door of my office and wept for five minutes straight. And for the next half hour, we went on to behave like raving children.

—Steffie

SYNERGISTIC PARTNERSHIPS

Working in effective alliances assumes that both parties bring something useful and needed to the partnership. Effective alliances also create synergy, that is, the partnership has more power than the two individuals acting separately. Effective alliances are not necessarily always harmonious, but they do transcend differences, create new options, and yield productive work.

Since business is still a male environment, the challenge for women in the business world is finding a way to operate successfully without losing our footing as women. For example, Carolyn had to learn how to stick to her values but develop the versatility to use the communication style that works with the person she's talking to. This is just as necessary with male friends and lovers as it is with male work colleagues.

Here are some warning signs that the situation *isn't* working for you:

- You find yourself devaluing women and what they bring to the workplace.

- You feel chronically angry or worthless.

- You feel as if you must be more like a man (more decisive, commanding, assertive) to get ahead or get along, in ways that compromise your true self.

- You feel that your only choice is to leave the organization or relationship in search of a more hospitable situation.

POWER AND STATUS

To start our exploration of power and status, look at the following graphic, which shows the elements involved in completing any kind of task. (Thanks again to Peter G. Ossorio, Ph.D., for the conceptual basis for this model.)

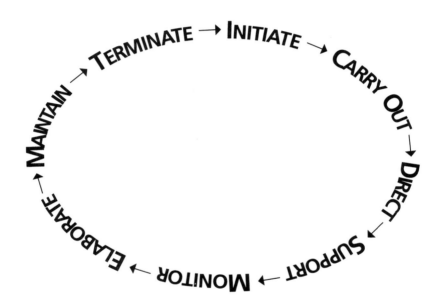

All the elements are familiar and obvious. When more than one person is involved, these tasks are typically broken out into roles. This is the way they are most often divided:

High Profile	Low Profile
Initiate	Carry out
Direct	Support
Monitor	Elaborate
Terminate	Maintain

We call the role on the left "High Profile" because it is usually more visible. The person in this role gives orders: start, stop, do it this way. The "Low Profile" supporting role is typically carried out behind the scenes. The person in this role performs the work and influences the way it is done— or not done. It is critical to realize that *power does not mean visibility*. Regardless of visibility, both roles are essential for getting the job done, hence equally powerful. If the High Profile person gives orders and nobody carries them out, nothing gets done. Think of a sit-down strike, or the boss who doesn't have the skills to do the work he or she has just ordered to be done.

Just as power is not about visibility, it is also not the same as status. In our culture we give the High Profile role higher status; more perks (the office with the view, the parking space by the door) are attached to it. The Low Profile role is low-status; the person who is "just" a secretary does this work and eats in the cafeteria. But the boss cannot get along without the secretary.

The High Profile role has traditionally been given to men, and the Low Profile role to women. Nevertheless, both men and women have proved themselves capable of assuming either role and can gain enormous power by switching roles, as needed, to get the job done.

Swapping roles can take a little practice. It is hard for men to move into Low Profile positions, because they are reluctant to do something that is seen as low-status or feminine. Women, on the other hand, are accustomed to being in Low Profile positions and generally are not as concerned as men are with status. We may be uncomfortable moving into High Profile positions because we are accustomed to making requests rather than giving orders. But we are used to giving orders to kids, so why not adults? Even though we have historically been trapped in these Low Profile roles, learning to play both roles gives us more choices and greater flexibility.

We are breaking cultural stereotypes here. It is particularly hard for men to accept a woman in a High Profile role, even if you have demonstrated your ability to play it and been authorized to do so. If you've been called a "castrating bitch" when you stepped in to give orders, this could be why. (It's happened to us!) Women may not like this role either. We've found that moving in with a pleasant, nurturing style may create less resistance in the beginning. Then we can move into a more directive mode.

TACTICS FOR USING POWER WISELY

- You don't have to take all the power all the time, only what you need at the moment. Grabbing all the power prevents others from contributing with enthusiasm. Men will become competitive unless you're willing to share the glory. Women will pull away and exclude you.

- When giving directions, you don't have to be harsh. Be encouraging, rather than commanding. Using softer language allows you to be more effective without losing control.

- Know the source of your power *from others' perspectives*. Is it competence? Position? Both? Don't make the mistake of assuming that you can move it to another arena. When renowned baby expert Dr. Spock attempted to be a spokesperson on the Vietnam War, for example, he was not seen as credible, because he was stepping out of his established realm of expertise.

- Take your stands on important issues early, to demonstrate your strength and courage. Make clear to others what your boundaries are. Show your willingness to back up your stand. In this way, you will be seen as powerful and authoritative.

THE FRESH LIGHT OF FEMININE VALUES

Women tend to feel disempowered when their subjective approach to problem solving is discredited. In the man's world, the objective approach has been traditionally put forth as superior, which is simply not true. Hang in there! There *is* logic in feelings, and they can be translated into logical language. Don't be bamboozled by masculine logic, and don't give up your ethical stance.

Feminine values are being accepted, even lauded, in the business world by well-known consultants such as Tom Peters (author of *Thriving on Chaos: A Handbook for a Management Revolution*, 1987). And in the business press, article after article on advances in business gives examples of bringing the feminine perspective in to revive corporations dying from the rigid, hierarchical, nonpeople-oriented structures that no longer get results—and worse, alienate employees. With the new emphasis on quality and speed, the old organizational pyramids are giving way to flatter, more flexible, and more egalitarian forms that include employees at all levels in making responsible decisions that affect the bottom line of the company. The old-time command-and-control style of management is being replaced by a more collegial, supportive approach that inspires rather than extracts excellence from workers. Similar changes are taking place in families.

These new approaches reflect the classic feminine values of caretaking, cooperation, and relationship building, and both men and women are capable of working in this way. A man who worked for a female CEO told us that the most important thing he learned from her was how to support and take care of employees. When a project was going wrong, she listened to what was bothering him, asked whether he had the support materials and personnel he needed, and even helped him make copies of papers to meet a deadline. Feeling nurtured instead of criticized, he responded in return with a willingness to do his best. This is an example of what Marilyn Loden and Judy B. Rosner found in their research on women and management styles, as mentioned in Chapter Three (see their book, *Workforce America*, 1991).

Observe what is happening around you so that you can speak out articulately and compellingly to preserve your values. Learn to speak from the heart with calm, linear thinking. Learn to discipline yourself emotionally. This doesn't mean denying your emotions, but expressing them in a way that will foster acceptance. So many women talk about learning to be "stone faces" in order to advance—never showing any kind of feeling at all because they see it makes men uncomfortable. Maybe being a little uncomfortable is good for them—and us. Just don't overwhelm anyone with emotion.

Be a pioneer; explore the potential application of women's values in business and political situations. Seek allies among men and women. Deliberately work to build connections with people who support you and agree with your goals and projects. Do your homework by talking to key men who are involved, one-on-one, behind the scenes. Seek a critic who is tough and who can work with you to help you refine your strategy for getting your ideas accepted.

Above all, it helps if you truly *like* men. Be affectionate, caring, and nurturing. Capitalize on your natural instincts to take care of team members, both male and female.

Payoffs for Versatility

▶ Effective alliances with men yield greater job opportunities.

▶ As a wise woman, you are able to be effective in a much broader community.

▶ You rise to a position of power and influence.

▶ You introduce feminine values into the masculine system.

▶ You gain respect and have self-respect.

▶ You become a force to be reckoned with.

▶ You wield power effectively, rather than letting it control you.

Alliances for Action

Salty Welborn is an influential director of a community hospital. When she took over as the acting chair of the board of directors and head of the hospital, she immediately established her power. There were roughly thirty men and only three women on the board, and it was run in a typical "old boys' club" fashion: behind-the-scenes maneuvering, informal agreements to consistently support certain people, and ignored input from the women. The board had been off-course and floundering for some time. Salty had tried every direct means of influencing the board, to no avail. When the hospital reached a real crisis point, she adopted the board's own tactics. First she called each board member to determine who her allies were. Sure that she had strong support, she rounded up enough votes to elect a complete slate of new officers at the next meeting—and did it. As the new president, in classic male style, she turned the tables on the group by saying pleasantly, "Now, boys, we're going to play by

my rules." Then she made it clear that her "rules" were about integrity, caring for people, and living up to a standard of commitment to the community. All heads in the room nodded. She proceeded to capitalize on her ability to use just as much power as she needed to, and asked others to execute decisions using *their* expertise.

Her versatility emerged further when she and others were concerned about a specific project that was becoming a significant financial drain on the hospital. The issue got the attention of the male board members because of the immediate short-term cash problem it caused. The women on the board were more concerned about the long-term implications for the hospital's ability to grow—that is, how it affected the mission and purpose of the organization.

Salty appealed to the male and female board members according to their individual biases. She is brilliant at directing, making good use of people, and making them feel valued. Her power comes through her clear vision, her authenticity, and the commitment she inspires in others.

TOOLS OF EMPOWERMENT

Exercise *CLUES FROM THE MOVIES*

Rent some movie videos and use them as learning tools by exploring the following issues:

1. *Out of Africa* is about a woman who made it in a man's world and also survived in a physically hostile environment.
   Consider what the Baroness von Blixen values, what ideals she is committed to. Where is she effective? Ineffective? Watch for the masculine and feminine perspectives being played out: (a) in Karen's relationship with Denys, (b) in the beach picnic scene, (c) in the breakup, and (d) when she goes to the governor to get land for the native people.

2. *Working Girl* features Sigourney Weaver as an honorary male in conflict with Melanie Griffith as a character who questions but doesn't forfeit her feminine values.
   Notice how Griffith's character (Tess McGill) does her homework and becomes competent, how she maintains her relationships with co-workers, how hurt she is by her boss's betrayal (men do it all the time to each other, but women don't expect it), and how she succeeds by persevering without being strident or overbearing, unlike her boss Katherine Parker (Sigourney Weaver).

3. In *Wildcats,* Goldie Hawn plays a football coach who is challenged to produce a winning team and to retain the custody of her children. She succeeds at both tasks without losing her feminine values, learning in the process where to draw the line and where to take a stand. She is a woman who leads with her heart, not her head.
   Observe how Hawn clarifies her values and goals, how she keeps her relationship with her sister as a reality

check for her own goals, how she gains the respect of the school principal and the young men she is coaching (maintaining her humor, persevering, and participating in the "marathon"), and how, in the scene in which she asks her husband to back off on the custody issue, taking a stand gets her what she wants—and how she gives that up in the courtroom scene.

4. *The Color Purple* is a story about some Southern black women who become liberated from both their circumstances and their limiting concepts of themselves. They are examples of vision, patience, determination, and courage.

   Notice how the character Celie and her sister develop their sense of who they are and the courage to act on it through mutual support and commitment to a common goal—maintaining their relationship through the years and across the ocean. They also discover themselves through this commitment to their relationship. During the dinner scene when the adult Celie (Whoopi Goldberg) announces that she is leaving, pay attention to the powerful, yet indirect, ways in which the women support and affirm each other and the resulting courage each gains to seek what she as an individual wants in her life.

Exercise   *FINDING THE FEELINGS IN FACTS*

Using specific, concrete, action-oriented masculine-style communication can be just as persuasive as talking about your feelings. When you use language your audience can relate to, it enhances your effectiveness, without requiring you to be untrue to yourself. The following exercise, created by H. Joel Jeffrey, Ph.D., gives you some practice "translating":

1. Pick a topic you feel strongly about (women in business, the proper way to raise children, and so on). Write down four or five statements that express how you feel and how important this is to you.

2. Select three specific facts, ideas, or concrete actions that symbolize your feelings about the issue. For example:

Issue: Equality in the workplace

Feelings: Angry, indignant, determined

Specifics: Sixty-five percent of the entering workforce in the year 2000 will be women.

              Women bring a different set of strengths to business.

              Business faces big challenges that it can meet more effectively by using both men's and women's strengths.

3. Write a two-minute speech in which you talk about these specifics (*not* your feelings about them). Give the speech—to the mirror, to a female friend, and to a male friend.

4. Now go back and note where your speech reveals your values or helps to promote them. When you spot an instance of this, write it down.

5. Go to each friend and ask, "I feel this way about this issue. Did that come across to you? Did I communicate my feelings to you?" Note where you got your feelings across and where you didn't. Revise your speech, with your friends' help, still being careful not to put in "feeling" words. Instead, communicate feeling through emphasis and tone of voice.

Exercise   *SURVIVING MIXED-GENDER GROUPS*

If you are a woman who has lived primarily in an all-woman world and now wishes to move into mixed-gender groups, this will be a challenging, exciting experience, calling on you to grow and be your best. Here are some tips that should help you during the transition:

1. Mixed-gender groups operate according to male rules. You are in a foreign land. Don't be fooled; without realizing it, even the most powerful women in mixed-gender groups will abdicate to the male way of operating. Don't assume that what has worked before will work here. Don't expect harmony and consensus to be valued or individual points of view to be protected. Do expect a faster pace and a more

factual approach. Process will not be highly regarded; task is the focus of the group. Expect to be interrupted and ignored when you speak.

2. Find someone who can brief you on the group from an insider's perspective. Let your credentials be known as soon as possible; take the reins and don't be modest. Learn to play politics—trade, bargain, make deals, negotiate. Read *You Just Don't Understand* (Tannen, 1990), *Feminine Leadership or How to Succeed in Business Without Being One of the Boys* (Loden, 1985), *Leadership Secrets of Attila the Hun* (Roberts, 1985), *The Art of War* (Tzu, 1963), or *Liar's Poker* (Lewis, 1989) to better understand the male perspective. Spend time learning, listening, and observing.

3. Go back to women's groups in order to seek nurturing when you need it.

Knowing how to maximize gender differences in social and professional settings is a trump card for the empowered woman. It illustrates a high level of comfort with our own nature, as well as respect for the unique strengths of others. Versatility is a key component of building productive relationships with a wide variety of people.

Part Three

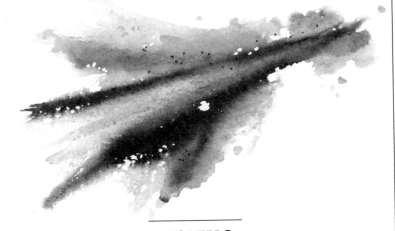

MOVING

FORWARD

17

Last Thoughts on the Journey

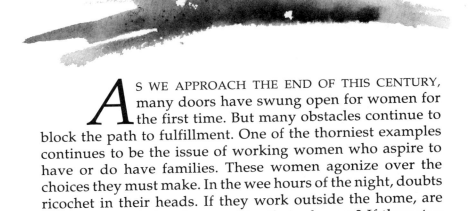

*A*S WE APPROACH THE END OF THIS CENTURY, many doors have swung open for women for the first time. But many obstacles continue to block the path to fulfillment. One of the thorniest examples continues to be the issue of working women who aspire to have or do have families. These women agonize over the choices they must make. In the wee hours of the night, doubts ricochet in their heads. If they work outside the home, are their children being damaged by their absence? If they stay home, are they harming themselves professionally or failing to make a contribution by their absence in the workplace?

These are the tough questions of our times. The world is changing, but it clearly has not changed enough. We need to fight for greater respect in the professional world for motherhood, for families. So many things could be done: on-site day care; more at-home work options; bonuses in the form of time off or paid day care for children, elderly parents, or invalids; corporate encouragement and support for greater participation in child-rearing by fathers; and so on. Businesses must acknowledge and incorporate the realities of people's lives in the workplace. Our difficulties must inspire us to resolve the enormous social issues that confront and confound us.

This book has suggested a first step: acknowledging that it is impossible to do it all, all at once. We have to make hard choices. Carolyn shares her experience: "When my family was young, I reached a point in my career where I had become a respected expert on stepfamilies. At that moment I had a chance to travel as a national speaker on the topic. While I was passionate about my work, I knew it would damage my family for me to follow that course. I decided to trust that I would have another chance to do something significant later in life, and I gave up that exciting opportunity, choosing instead to continue to pursue my private practice. While I feel very gratified by how my life has evolved, I also recognize the actual professional loss and the risk I took."

What we women must do is to engage in ongoing personal strategic planning. We have to take a long view of our lives and decide what choices we want to make now and later, to anticipate when we might take time out to focus on motherhood or an important calling, or time out to focus on our careers. The harsh truth is that we have to make sacrifices. We can't play all the roles at once.

Then we must express our hearts and minds and communicate our wishes. The responsibility for transforming our culture belongs to all of us and each of us has a right to an authentic and peaceful existence.

Achieving harmony is an ongoing process, a quest to possess and to cultivate the facets of empowerment. The empowered women whose lives inspired this book possessed the qualities of *authenticity, risk taking, vision, health, humor, harmony, receptivity, accountability, contentment, graciousness, alignment, communication,* and *versatility.* We all can invoke these qualities as we proceed to lead a life marked by authentic choices.

We have offered you a broad set of possibilities to think about and to take action on. Obviously, we do not encourage you to tackle them all simultaneously—or even ever. Use your discrimination as you decide upon a game plan. Take a personal inventory of your own empowerment. Pick out two or three facets of empowerment that you would like to work on. Reread those chapters, and choose some exercises to help you explore those qualities further. Think about sharing the process with a friend. Look for opportunities in your daily life in which you can practice using these qualities. Don't forget to celebrate your growth and progress! Finally, bear in mind that when you are in a place of authentic "being," the "doing" comes.

We hope we have encouraged you to embrace the incredible challenge of being a woman today—to make the tough choices while striving to honor your highest priorities, those things that bring the greatest meaning and fulfillment to your life. We wish you *contemplation* to reflect upon your personal truth, *commitment* to work toward what you value, *conviction* to say no and to say yes, and *courage* to grow, to dream, and to live a harmonious and empowered life.

BIBLIOGRAPHY

Astin, Helen S., and Carole Leland. *Women of Influence, Women of Vision: A Cross-Generational Study of Leaders of Social Change.* San Francisco: Jossey-Bass, 1991.

Autry, James A. *Love and Profit.* New York: William Morrow, 1991.

Baldwin, Christina. *One to One: Self-Understanding Through Journal Writing.* New York: M. Evans, 1977.

Bateson, Mary Catherine. *Composing a Life.* New York: Atlantic Monthly Press, 1989.

Belenky, Mary Field, Blythe McVicker Clinchy, Nancy Rule Goldberger, and Jill Mattuck Tarule. *Women's Ways of Knowing.* New York: Basic Books, 1986.

Blackman, Ann, Priscilla Painton, and Elizabeth Taylor. "The War Against Feminism," *Time*, March 9, 1992.

Bolen, Jean Shinoda. *Goddesses in Everywoman: A New Psychology of Women.* New York: Harper & Row, 1984.

Bolen, Jean Shinoda. *Gods in Everyman: A New Psychology of Men's Lives and Loves.* New York: Harper & Row, 1989.

Bolton, Robert. *People Skills: How to Assert Yourself, Listen to Others and Resolve Conflicts.* New York: Simon & Schuster, 1979.

Cousins, Norman. *Anatomy of an Illness.* New York: Bantam Books, 1982.

Depree, Max. *Leadership Is an Art.* New York: Doubleday, 1989.

Frankl, Viktor. *Man's Search for Meaning.* Boston: Beacon Press, 1959.

Gilligan, Carol. *In a Different Voice.* Cambridge, Mass.: Harvard University Press, 1982.

Goldberg, Natalie. *Writing Down the Bones: Freeing the Writer Within.* Boston: Shambala Publications, 1986.

Grindler, John, and Richard Bandler. *Transformation,* ed. by Connierae Andreas. Moab, Utah: Real People Press, 1981.

Hagberg, Janet O. *Real Power.* San Francisco: Harper & Row, 1984.

Harris, Maria. *Dance of the Spirit: The Seven Steps of Women's Spirituality.* New York: Bantam Books, 1989.

Hayes, Peter. *The Supreme Adventure: The Experience of Siddha Yoga.* New York: Delta, 1988.

Helgeson, Sally. *The Female Advantage: Women's Ways of Leadership.* New York: Doubleday Currency, 1990.

Hirsch, Sandra, and Jean Kummerow. *LifeTYPES.* New York: Warner Books, 1989.

Holland, Dorothy C., and Margaret A. Eisenhart. *Educated in Romance: Women, Achievement, and College Culture.* Chicago: University of Chicago Press, 1990.

Jacklin, Carol, and Eleanor Maccoby. *The Psychology of Sex Differences.* Stanford, Calif.: Stanford University Press, 1974.

Johnston, William B., and Arnold H. Packer. *Workforce America: Work and Workers for the 21st Century.* Indianapolis: Hudson Institute, 1987.

Lewis, Michael. *Liar's Poker.* New York: Penguin Books, 1989.

Lindbergh, Anne Morrow. *Gift from the Sea.* New York: Vintage Books, 1975.

Loden, Marilyn. *Feminine Leadership or How to Succeed in Business Without Being One of the Boys.* New York: Random House, 1985.

Loden, Marilyn, and Judy B. Rosner. *Workforce America: Managing Diversity as a Vital Resource.* Chicago: Business One Irwin, 1991.

Maccoby, Eleanor E. "Gender and Relationships: A Developmental Account," *American Psychologist*, April 1990.

Mehrabian, Albert. "Communication Without Words," *Psychology Today*, Vol. 2, No. 4, September 1968.

Miller, Jean Baker. *Toward a New Psychology of Women.* Boston: Beacon Press, 1986.

Ossorio, Peter G. *Clinical Topics.* LRI Report No. 11. Boulder, Colo.: LRI Associates, 1976.

Peters, Tom. *Thriving on Chaos: A Handbook for a Management Revolution.* New York: Harper Perennial, 1987.

Rainer, Tristine. *The New Diary: How to Use a Journal for Self-Guidance and Expanded Creativity.* Los Angeles: Jeremy P. Tarcher, 1978.

Roberts, Wess. *Leadership Secrets of Attila the Hun.* New York: Warner Books, 1985.

Roddick, Anita. *Body and Soul: Profits with Principles—The Amazing Success Story of Anita Roddick and The Body Shop.* New York: Crown Publishers, 1991.

Rosner, Judy B. "Ways Women Lead," *Harvard Business Review*, November–December 1990.

[Rosner, Judy B.]. "Debate: Ways Men and Women Lead." *Harvard Business Review*, January–February 1991. [Responses to Rosner 1990 and her reply.]

Sidel, Ruth. *On Her Own: Growing Up in the Shadow of the American Dream.* New York: Penguin Books, 1990.

Simmons, George R., and G. Deborah Weissman. *Men and Women: Partners at Work.* Los Altos, Calif.: Crisp Publications, 1990.

Simon, Sidney. *Getting Unstuck: Breaking Through Your Barriers to Change.* New York: Warner Books, 1988.

Tannen, Deborah. *You Just Don't Understand: Women and Men in Conversation*. New York: William Morrow, 1990.

Titus, Meredith, A., and William H. Smith. "Contemporary Issues in the Psychotherapy of Women," *Bulletin of the Menninger Clinic*, Vol. 56, No. 1, Winter 1992, pp. 48–61.

Tzu, Sun. *The Art of War*. Oxford: Oxford University Press, 1963.

Walker, Lenore E. *The Battered Woman*. New York: Harper & Row, 1979.

Walker, Lenore E. *Terrifying Love: Why Battered Women Kill and How Society Responds*. New York: Harper & Row, 1989.

Ziegler, Warren. *A Mindbook of Exercises for Futures-Inventors*. Denver, Colo.: Futures-Invention Associates, 1982.

SOURCES FOR QUOTATIONS

The Home Book of Quotations. Selected by Burton Stevenson. New York: Greenwich House, 1984.

The International Thesaurus of Quotations. Compiled by Rhoda Thomas Tripp. New York: Harper & Row, 1970.

1,911 Best Things Anybody Ever Said. Selected and compiled by Robert Byrne. New York: Fawcett Columbine, 1988.

The Oxford Dictionary of Modern Quotations. Oxford: Oxford University Press, 1991.

The Oxford Dictionary of Quotations. Oxford: Oxford University Press, 1980.

The Quotable Woman. Philadelphia: Running Press, 1991.

Shaef, Anne Wilson. *Meditations for Women Who Do Too Much*. San Francisco: Harper & Row, 1990.

Winokur, Jon, Ed. *A Curmudgeon's Garden of Love*. New York: New American Books, 1989.

INDEX

The Athena Group

The Athena Group is a leadership training and consulting company created to promote working environments where men and women are empowered to work together as equals and where differences are honored and understood. Since the company was founded in 1989, we have worked extensively with women, attuning ourselves to their concerns, their potential contributions, and their perspectives on the obstacles and opportunities they face. Our leadership program for women is designed to make women proud of who they are and aware of the power that comes from being their authentic selves. To date, we have trained nearly one thousand women in middle and upper management.

We have also researched the differences in how men and women operate in the workplace and have developed a series of training programs and consulting interventions for fostering partnership, teamwork, and productive working relationships. We help clients assess the current organizational climate and the company's readiness to initiate change. We identify the "glass ceiling" and "glass wall" elements within the organization and offer recommendations for ways to disassemble them. We also suggest specific techniques to integrate gender-based differences into the organizational structures of the company. Finally, we train employees in recognizing and dealing with the differences between men and women and show how those differences affect such things as work focus, decision making, and relationships.

In all of our work, we are committed to establishing a work environment where all people are empowered to perform at the peak of their abilities—one where the entire work force of the next century can truly thrive.

ORDER FORM

QTY.	TITLE	PRICE	TOTAL
_____	*Doing It All Isn't Everything:* *A Woman's Guide to Harmony* *and Empowerment*		
_____	Hardcover edition (6×9, 208 pages)	$19.95	_____
_____	Paperback edition (6×9, 208 pages)	12.95	_____

Texas residents add 7.25% sales tax + _____

Shipping and Handling
($2.00 for 1st book, $1.00 per book thereafter) +   + _____

TOTAL [   ]

**Quantity Discounts
are available
for training programs
and other company uses.
Call 512-266-2112
for information.**

☐ Please contact me about
The Athena Group's
workshops and services.

☐ Payment enclosed.
Please make checks payable to New Perspectives Press.

Name _____

Organization _____

Address _____

City _____ State _____ Zip _____

Phone (____) _____

Signature _____

☐ MasterCard ☐ VISA
Card No. _____
Exp. Date _____

To place your order by phone, call
1-800-945-3132 or write to New
Perspectives Press, 5275 McCormick
Mountain Road, Austin, Texas 78734.